AF687336

MAKING TAX DIGITAL WITHOUT THE PANIC

HOW SOLE TRADERS AND LANDLORDS CAN BUILD SIMPLE SYSTEMS THAT JUST WORK

JUSTIN TURNER

A CIP catalogue record of this book is available from the British Library.

ISBN (Paperback): 978-1-7396720-4-1 Imprint: Independently published.

ISBN (EBook): 978-1-7396720-5-8 Imprint: Independently published.

For further information about this book, please contact the author at: www.askjt.co.uk.

For Benji, James, and Sue

CONTENTS

INTRODUCTION

People are making out that Making Tax Digital is a disaster. A quick browse on YouTube brings up thumbnails using words like *"nightmare"* or images of people with their heads in their hands. When I produced my own video on YouTube, I decided to take a different approach. I've never been a fan of catastrophising.

The problem with online videos is simple. People want clicks, and disasters and huge problems attract attention. That does not make them accurate. So this book takes a deliberately calm and positive view of Making Tax Digital. Not because the change is trivial, but because panic is rarely helpful.

Without blowing my own trumpet too much, I am probably one of the more experienced systems accountants in the UK. But what is a systems accountant? It is someone who can bridge business challenges with accounting expertise and a deep understanding of technology. My background starts with a degree in Information Systems in 2004. I then went on to form a web technologies business, which ran until around 2014. For over a decade, I worked on building software solutions for organisations such as Action Against Hunger. During that time, I became very comfortable with how systems are designed, how data moves, and how technology fails when it is bolted on rather than thought through.

After that, I saw a significant opportunity in accountancy. The Finance Act of 2015 introduced discussion around digital record keeping. New software providers entered the market and challenged long-established players. Cloud accounting platforms began talking about API connections and real-time data. While most people understandably ignored this detail, I recognised that these changes were laying the groundwork for something much bigger.

That "something bigger" is Making Tax Digital.

This is not just something I advise on professionally. I also have my own portfolio of rental properties, which means I am a landlord who will be reporting under Making Tax Digital myself.

Why This Is One Book, Not Two

So why haven't I written a separate book for landlords and sole traders? After all, for landlords it is described as extra reporting. For sole traders it is described as more admin. Both descriptions miss the point.

The reason this book covers both landlords and sole traders is simple. It is the same system. Yes, the income sources differ, but the mechanics, habits, and technology are identical.

Splitting this into two books would suggest there are two

different problems. There aren't. There is one system that needs to run quietly in the background, regardless of whether your income comes from rent, scaffolding, plumbing, marketing consulting, or bookkeeping.

That is the system this book is about.

We need to stop talking about Making Tax Digital as a problem. It is happening, and the more useful question is how to implement it well. That is what I aim to help you with in this book. Not just understanding the requirements, but building a clear and practical route to doing this properly.

When people describe MTD as a problem, they are often not really talking about the rules themselves. They are expressing a lack of trust in HMRC. Historically, HMRC has not always covered itself in glory, and there is understandable concern about implementing a change of this scale while other pressures remain.

But worrying about whether HMRC can cope is not productive. That is their problem. Your challenge is much simpler. You need to build a system that meets the requirements of Making Tax Digital and works reliably in the real world. In fact, this is not new for me.

We have been helping landlords and sole traders build digital bookkeeping systems for years. For larger landlords, that has meant real-time profit and loss reporting across portfolios. For sole traders, it has meant simple, reliable systems that work quietly in the background.

One of my clients, Tony, rang me recently and said, "This MTD thing, what needs to happen?"

The answer was simple.

"Nothing, Tony. You've already been set up for this for years."

FINAL WORD

Part 4 of this book focuses on being a sole trader, and Part 5 on being a landlord. I have experience in both areas, so it made sense to cover them in some detail. Not everyone has an accountant, and I wanted to include the kind of practical help you might not get unless you picked up this book. I have also shared some deeper thinking that other books on the market do not offer, often because the people writing them have not had to run these systems in practice.

Why mention the two different sections? Because some people have both types of income, rental and sole trade, and the system is fundamentally the same. If you do not have rental income or sole trader income, you can skip the relevant section. If you are a landlord and your friend John the plumber is a sole trader, you can always lend him the book.

You'll also find extra practical resources linked throughout the book.

Where it helps, I've included QR codes that take you to short podcast mini-series, step-by-step software setup guides, and practical worksheets, including a full worked example for landlords considering incorporation.

These resources let me show you things that are hard to explain clearly in print, like what "good" setup actually looks like inside real software, and how to apply the principles in this book to your own situation.

One final note on setup and registration.

You'll notice I've only included a small section in the penultimate chapter on how to register and get set up for Making Tax Digital. That's deliberate. HMRC pages change. Software menus move. Step-by-step screenshots date a book very quickly.

Instead, I've given you the principles and enough guidance to find the right pages yourself, without boring you with "click this, then click that" instructions that will be out of date by the time you read this.

The goal of this book is not to walk you through today's buttons.

It's to help you build a system that still works when those buttons move.

PART 1. WHO, WHAT, WHEN

1

WHY MAKING TAX DIGITAL IS NO LONGER OPTIONAL

For most people, Making Tax Digital (MTD) has been background noise. Like a fridge humming away in the kitchen. You know it's there. You hear it occasionally. But over time, you learn to tune it out.

MTD was announced. Then delayed. Then softened, tweaked, and trimmed. Each delay trained people to think, *"It's probably fine."* That instinct was understandable. But it is no longer valid.

This is no longer something that *might* happen. It **is** happening. Whether it's 2026 or 2027, the years when action is required are no longer theoretical. You need to do something now.

Why This Time Really Is Different

Making Tax Digital for Income Tax, or the rather catchy acronym you'll often see, MTD ITSA, is not a sudden change of direction.

Things started to shift around 2015, when HMRC set out

a clear long-term plan: digital records, digital reporting, and digital tax accounts. That direction was refined through successive Budgets and Finance Act updates between 2016 and 2017.

VAT went first, and I remember that change well. It was actually the impetus that put my accountancy firm, Orange Umbrella, on a road to growth.

I've had a VAT-registered business since 2004. I remember the green VAT100 form arriving in the post. I'd diligently fill it in with a pen and send it back with a cheque. God forbid I made a mistake, because then the Tippex had to come out.

So when digital record keeping arrived, I embraced it with open arms.

Back when I ran my software business, a bookkeeper would attend the office each month and spend an entire day on the books. When digital accounting really took hold, I implemented tools that first halved that support and later reduced it to just a couple of hours a month.

That's exciting! You reduce the time it takes to do a job, and that saves money. But Income Tax was always next.

The delays were not rewrites. They were technical pitstops. HMRC needed software providers, banks, and systems to catch up with the ambition. That work has now largely been done.

- **From April 2026**, hundreds of thousands of sole traders and landlords will legally join the system.
- **From April 2027 & 2028**, even more people will be pulled in.

HMRC stated in August 2025 that around seven million people have sole trader or landlord income. Around 2.9 million of those individuals will be brought into MTD reporting by April 2028. This change is being phased in between 2026 and 2028.

Very sensibly, you're reading this book because it will explain exactly **when** you will be affected and, more importantly, **how** you can deal with it.

There is no alternative system waiting in the wings. No fallback. No parallel route. Self Assessment, as most people understand it today, is being retired for these groups. For roughly 2.9 million people in the UK economy, this represents a major change.

No, HMRC Hasn't Invented a New Tax

This is where fear tends to creep in. We all know that so-called "tax adviser" called Mike who gives advice down the pub but actually works as a plumber. When people hear "Making Tax Digital", they often imagine higher tax bill, more inspections and more penalties

That is not what this is. In fact, if HMRC gets this right, we may see **more stable tax bills, fewer inspections**, and **fewer penalties**, simply because records are better.

The irony is that better bookkeeping often leads to **lower** tax bills, not higher ones.

Making Tax Digital does **not** change:

- Tax rates
- Allowable expenses
- Payment deadlines

You still pay tax on:

- 31st January (balancing payment and 1st payment on account)
- 31st July (2nd payment on account)

What does change is how information reaches HMRC. Instead of one annual snapshot taken under pressure, HMRC now wants a rolling picture built up over the year. That is uncomfortable if your records are chaotic. It is uneventful if your systems are clean and organised.

Why HMRC Is Pushing This Change

Making Tax Digital is often described as quarterly submissions. That is the visible part, not the purpose.

The real shift is away from annual catch-up.

For decades, the system encouraged people to:

- Leave record keeping until the end of the year
- Rely on memory
- Panic at deadlines

That approach created three problems for HMRC:

- Late information
- Poor data quality
- Reactive compliance

It also created stress, uncertainty, and unpleasant surprises for taxpayers. I decided to write this book at the start of February, straight after the January self assessment rush. Out of the 225 tax returns I submitted, around 85 were left by clients until January.

Imagine the horror when your accountant reviews your

records and tells you that not only did you breach the VAT threshold 14 months ago, but profits are up and you now have a £10,000 balancing payment, plus likely backdated VAT of £30,000.

Or the client who sent information too late and discovered they were over the pension taper threshold, had missed the scheme pays deadline, and now faced a £19,000 tax bill.

These are not hypothetical examples. These are things I dealt with this January.

So do I think quarterly reporting is a good idea?

Yes, I do. Because it allows us to remove some of that stress. MTD moves reporting from retrospective to current. We get real-time information about profits and likely tax. Work is spread across the year rather than crammed into one enormous push.

It feels uncomfortable at first. Done properly, it becomes simpler and calmer over time.

The Hidden Upside Most People Miss

Once records are kept digitally and updated regularly, something important happens. Automation starts to work.

- Bank feeds pull income and expenses in automatically
- Digital receipt scanning removes paperwork
- Mobile apps allow invoices and quotes to be raised on the road
- Instead of chasing information, you review it.
- Instead of guessing, you can see where you stand.

This is not more work. It is the same work, done earlier, with far less pressure, and supported by tools that actually give you useful information.

Why This Matters for Cash Flow

One of the quiet benefits of Making Tax Digital is visibility. When you know:

- What you've earned
- What you've spent
- What tax is building up
- Where cash has gone and how drawings affect cash flow

You make better decisions.

One of the biggest challenges I see is that it's relatively easy to build a profitable business, but much harder to live from that business properly. I regularly see clients spending money that should have been set aside for tax.

With better systems, we can spot these issues earlier. Over time, this may lead to something that sounds worrying but is often helpful: **more frequent tax payments.**

Smaller, regular payments are usually easier to manage than large, unpredictable bills. The government has said this won't happen until after 2029, but the direction of travel is clear.

For tradespeople affected by CIS, this could be genuinely transformative. Instead of long waits for refunds or sharp peaks and troughs, quarterly reporting could support:

- More frequent repayments
- Smoother cash flow
- Greater stability

That is not a burden. That is progress.

Personally, as a landlord, my last tax return showed much higher profits than the year before, which resulted in a significant payment on account. But because I already use software for my properties, I could see that I'd also had two large repairs. I was able to factor those in with confidence and reduce my payments on account without the risk of a penalty.

We're not there yet with changes to tax deadlines, but implementing proper software gives you control. And control changes how this feels.

End-of-Chapter Checklist

✅ I understand MTD is now unavoidable
✅ I know this is about systems, not tax rates
✅ I can see how the delays created false comfort
✅ I'm thinking about habits, not forms

2

WHO IS CAUGHT, WHEN, AND HOW HMRC DECIDES

This chapter answers three questions. Most confusion around Making Tax Digital comes from mixing three things together:

- Does this apply to me?
- When does it start?
- How does HMRC decide?

So we won't. We will take them one at a time, slowly and clearly.

The Thresholds, Clearly Stated

Making Tax Digital for Income Tax is triggered by **gross income**, not profit. That means the total amount you invoice or receive **before** expenses are deducted.

The thresholds are:

From April 2026

- Sole traders and landlords with **gross income over £50,000**

From April 2027

- Sole traders and landlords with **gross income over £30,000**

From April 2028

- Sole traders and landlords with **gross income over £20,000**

If your gross income is below **£20,000**, you are not in scope "**yet**". That word matters. *Yet* still leaves over **4 million** landlords and sole traders outside the system. Around **1.6 million** landlords and sole traders sit in the **£10,001 to £19,999** gross income band, so it is entirely possible HMRC may decide it is worthwhile to bring this group into scope in the future.

What Counts as Income

This is another area where people get caught out. For Making Tax Digital, HMRC looks at:

- Self-employed trading income
- UK rental income
- Overseas rental income, if it is taxable in the UK

It does **not** look at:

- Wages
- Dividends
- Pensions

Unless you also have trading or property income.

> *If you are* ***both*** *a sole trader* ***and*** *a landlord, HMRC looks at your* ***combined non-PAYE income.***

This surprises people. Two income streams that felt separate under Self Assessment are treated as one total for MTD purposes.

Turnover Versus Profit

HMRC deliberately uses **turnover**, not profit.

It does this because:

- Turnover is harder to manipulate
- Profit depends on judgement
- Systems need simple thresholds

This can feel unfair if you have high costs. But HMRC is not measuring success. It is deciding whether you must use a particular reporting system. Once you separate eligibility from performance, the logic becomes easier to accept.

How HMRC Decides

This is where assumptions creep in. HMRC does not guess. It does not estimate. It does not ask politely.

It checks **already filed tax returns.** Specifically, it looks at your income from **two tax years earlier.**

That return determines whether you must join Making Tax Digital. This rule is explained in detail in Chapter 3, because it causes more frustration than any other part of the system.

What Happens If Your Income Drops

This is important. If your income drops after HMRC has decided you are in scope, you generally stay in. There is no automatic exit just because business is quieter or costs increase. Making Tax Digital is about **how you report**, not **how well you are doing.**

If your income falls from £50,000 to £39,000, HMRC knows you are likely to re-enter the system in 2027 anyway, so opting you out serves little purpose.

Earlier in this chapter, we mentioned the 1.6 million sole traders and landlords in the £10,000 to £20,000 bracket. Over the long term, this strategy gives HMRC ongoing visibility without constant entry and exit from the system.

Letters From HMRC

If HMRC believes you are in scope, they will write to you. That letter is not an invitation. It is a notice. By the time it arrives, the decision has already been made.

A common mistake is assuming the letter *starts* the process. In reality, it ends it.

What to Do Now

You do not need to panic.
But you should:

- Check your historic **gross income**, not profit
- Understand **when** you are likely to be caught
- Stop assuming HMRC will take personal context into account

HMRC applies rules **consistently**, not sympathetically. Good systems make that irrelevant.

End-of-Chapter Checklist

✅ I know which income HMRC looks at
✅ I understand the thresholds and dates
✅ I know turnover, not profit, matters
✅ I understand how HMRC decides eligibility

3

THE TWO-YEAR LOOK-BACK RULE THAT CATCHES PEOPLE OUT

The look-back rule is responsible for more confusion and more frustration than almost any other part of Making Tax Digital. It is also non-negotiable. HMRC applies it exactly as written, every time. Let's establish the facts.

~

How HMRC Decides If Making Tax Digital Applies to You

HMRC does not look at what you earn this year. It does not look at what you expect to earn next year. It does not care if your income has dropped recently. Instead, HMRC looks backwards. Specifically, it looks at your **gross income** from two tax years earlier.

If that figure is above the threshold, you are in.

This applies to:

- Sole traders
- Landlords

- People who have both self-employment and rental income

There is no averaging.There is no discretion. There is no appeal based on fairness.

A Real-World Example

Let's say you are a landlord, but these numbers could equally be the sales for a sole trader.

- **2023/24** rental income: £52,000
- **2024/25** rental income: £28,000

Your instinctive reaction is obvious:

> ***"I'm under the threshold now, so this shouldn't apply to me."***

But HMRC disagrees.

How HMRC Decides When You Join

Your 2023/24 tax return, filed in January 2025, is what determines whether you must join Making Tax Digital from April 2026. I've used a landlord example here, but the rule is exactly the same for a sole trader. The only difference is that instead of rent, HMRC looks at your turnover, in plain English, how much you sold.

Once you are in, you generally stay in.

You should already have received a letter from HMRC

confirming this. Unless you stop renting, cease trading altogether, or qualify for a specific exemption, this change now applies to you.

There are a few specific exemptions from Making Tax Digital. You do not need to join if you have no UK self-employment or rental income, or if you are non-UK resident and only declare foreign income. HMRC may also accept applications for exemption on reasonable grounds, such as a disability preventing digital record keeping or other exceptional circumstances. If you believe you qualify, you must notify HMRC as exemptions are not automatic.

Why HMRC Does It This Way

HMRC needs certainty. It cannot base system access on estimates, intentions, or expectations. It needs filed, verified numbers. That is why HMRC uses historic tax returns. From HMRC's point of view, this approach makes perfect sense. From the taxpayer's point of view, it can feel disconnected from reality.

The Common Mistake

The most common mistake I see is this:

"I'll wait and see if I'm affected."

By the time HMRC writes to you, the decision has already been made and the clock is already running.

If your 2023/2024 or 2024/2025 return puts you over the line, April 2026 may be just around the corner, or it may already have passed by the time you are reading this. The same is true for those coming in from April 2027 or April 2028. The principle does not change. Know your numbers and take action now, rather than waiting for a letter and leaving yourself little or no time to respond.

For many people, this is a huge change. It requires a mindset shift. You need time to understand software, register accounts, and learn a completely new process. That is exactly why you must not wait.

What to Do Instead

You do not need to overhaul your life tomorrow.

But you should do three things now:

- Check your 2023/24 and 2024/25 gross income, not profit
- Assume HMRC will apply the rules exactly as written
- Build your systems early, while nothing is urgent

If your rental income or turnover was under £50,000 on your 2023/24 tax return but over £30,000 on your 2024/25 tax return, you will not be required to join Making Tax Digital from April 2026, but you should expect to be pulled in from April 2027.

If you are reading this book in a later tax year and find that you were under £30,000 in one year but over the next lower threshold in the following year, the same principle applies. HMRC will use the most recent completed tax return that crosses the entry threshold to decide when you join Making Tax Digital. The numbers may change over time, but the logic does not.

This book exists so you can take action calmly, cheaply, and without panic.

> ***If you have never used bookkeeping software before and discover you have a year to prepare, start using it now so you are ready well before the deadline.***

End-of-Chapter Checklist

- ✅ I know which tax year HMRC uses to test eligibility
- ✅ I understand that turnover, not profit, matters
- ✅ I know whether April 2026 applies to me
- ✅ I have stopped assuming HMRC will "see sense"

PART 2. WHAT ACTUALLY CHANGES IN REAL LIFE

4

FROM ANNUAL PANIC TO QUARTERLY HABITS

My friend Nasser has been a sole trader for decades, and I've been doing his tax returns for twelve years. So you might assume he's a ninja when it comes to Self Assessment.

Yet on deadline day, I texted him and said, "There's a risk you might be the last tax return we submit."

Nasser didn't go into business because he loved paperwork or tax returns. He went into business because he's excellent at what he does. And that's the point.

> ***Most people are not bad at tax. They are bad at organisation.***

And for years, the system has quietly told them that this is fine.

Under Self Assessment, you could file your tax return up to 31st January following the end of the tax year. In practice, that meant nearly ten months of breathing space.

There was no penalty for ignoring records for months, as long as everything was reconstructed by January. With enough late nights, caffeine, and mild panic, most people could recover.

That created a predictable pattern:

- Delay felt rational
- Batching felt efficient
- Last-minute effort felt heroic

From a behavioural point of view, this makes perfect sense. Humans respond to deadlines, not intentions. We act when consequences are close, not when they are distant.

Making Tax Digital changes that. It removes the annual safety net. It exposes timing problems that were always there. That is why MTD feels uncomfortable. Not because it is harder, but because problems surface sooner.

This chapter explains why that discomfort is normal, and how to adapt by changing when work happens, not by turning your life into a bookkeeping exercise.

The Old Rhythm

Self Assessment created a very specific behaviour pattern. For many people, it looked like this:

- Ignore paperwork
- Accumulate receipts
- Feel guilty
- Panic in December or January
- Hand everything over
- Forget about it again

This approach was inefficient. But it was familiar. And familiarity feels safe, even when it causes stress.

Why Quarterly Reporting Changes Everything

Quarterly reporting does not mean "doing tax four times a year".

It means:

- Looking at your numbers regularly
- Correcting small errors early
- Seeing tax build gradually instead of arriving as a shock

On paper, that sounds sensible. In practice, it can feel intrusive if you're not used to it. The discomfort comes from frequency, not complexity.

I wrote a whole book called The Science of Business, much of which explored social science and human behaviour. In particular, why we resist change. Some people reading this chapter will feel angry that HMRC is making them do this. That reaction is understandable.

But anger and resentment are unhelpful forces in a business. Understanding is far more productive.

~

When the Numbers Make the Decision

I was lucky enough to get on the property ladder in my early twenties. After eight years living in that house, I moved on, but I kept it as a rental.

After the first eighteen months, I wanted to see how the

property was performing. I logged into my bookkeeping system and ran a profit and loss report.

The yield was poor, so I sold it.

No emotion. It had been a home once. Now it was a business asset that was not performing, so it had to go.

The example of my former home, and the decision I made, highlights why we should not resist MTD. I used the same software to assess the yield that can now help you make informed business decisions, as well as submit your quarterly MTD returns.

The Myth of "More Work"

A common fear is that Making Tax Digital quadruples the workload. In practice, the opposite is often true. Under annual reporting:

- Work is batched
- Errors pile up
- Fixes are rushed

Under quarterly reporting:

- Work is lighter
- Problems are smaller
- Fixes are easier

The total effort often falls. The effort is simply spread out. As you saw in my rental property example, answers are easy to see in real time.

. . .

Why Habits Matter More Than Intelligence

Making Tax Digital does not reward people who understand tax. It rewards people who build habits. That can be uncomfortable for high-performing people who are used to:

- Bursting into action under pressure
- Solving problems late
- Moving on quickly

Ironically, I'm that kind of person. I thrive on deadlines and pressure. That's how books like this come into being.

But MTD favours:

- Short, regular check-ins
- Simple routines
- Boring consistency

While I enjoy deadlines, I also value control. I can log into our accounting software and see a live profit & loss for my accountancy firm at any time. We're three days past our VAT quarter end and my colleague has already emailed me our VAT liability, more than a month before payment is due.

That's control. No panic required. Quarterly income tax reporting may feel alien, but that level of visibility is a huge benefit.

The Mistake People Make

Many people assume they must do everything perfectly each quarter. **That isn't required.** Quarterly updates are updates, not final answers. HMRC accepts estimates. Adjustments happen later. Perfection at this stage is wasted energy.

What HMRC Actually Expects Each Quarter

Each quarterly update needs to answer one simple question:

> ***Roughly how much money came in and went out?***

That's it.

Not:

- Capital allowances
- Complex adjustments
- Clever planning

Those belong at year end. You may choose to do adjustments quarterly to produce accurate management accounts, but it's not a disaster if you don't. MTD helps you see what's coming. It does not lock you in. Once you view it this way, the pressure drops.

How People Who Adapt Early Feel

This is worth stating clearly. People who adapt early:

- Feel more in control
- Stop fearing tax bills
- Make better decisions during the year

They stop being surprised. Tax stops being something

that happens to them. It becomes something they can see coming.

End-of-Chapter Checklist

☑ I understand why quarterly reporting feels uncomfortable

☑ I know this is about habits, not intelligence

☑ I understand quarterly updates do not need perfection

☑ I can see how regular visibility reduces stress

5

WHAT HMRC REALLY MEANS BY "DIGITAL RECORDS"

This is where most people go wrong. They hear "digital records" and assume it means one of three things:

- Submitting numbers online instead of on paper
- Scanning receipts at the end of the year
- Using Excel instead of a notebook

None of those, on their own, meet the requirement. I see this misunderstanding every year. A client will tell me they've "gone digital", and what they usually mean is that they've recreated everything electronically just before the deadline. That feels modern, but it isn't what Making Tax Digital is asking for.

So let's be precise.

What a Digital Record Actually Is

A digital record is not the submission you send to

HMRC. It is the information that sits underneath it. Think of it as the building blocks, not the finished report.

For income, a digital record means capturing:

- The date the income was received
- The amount
- Where it came from

For expenses, it means recording:

- The date of the expense
- The amount
- Who you paid
- What it was for

The important point is not the list. It's **how the information exists.** That data must:

- Be created or captured in a digital form
- Be stored digitally, not reconstructed later
- Flow digitally into your quarterly updates

If you are typing figures into a spreadsheet at the end of the quarter from bank statements or paper receipts, you are not keeping digital records. You are recreating them.

And if you are manually typing data into spreadsheets, it is also costing you money. Time is one of the most valuable resources a business owner has.

A proper digital record is created once, at the point the transaction happens, and then reused. That is what Making Tax Digital is trying to achieve.

Later in the book, when we get onto implementation, I'll

talk about bank feeds and how data can flow automatically through software without repeated handling.

HMRC is not interested in beautifully presented spreadsheets or carefully written explanations. It wants structured data that can be traced.

Digital Records vs Digital Submission

This distinction matters. You can submit something digitally and still be non-compliant. For example:

- Typing totals into HMRC's portal
- Copying figures from a spreadsheet into software
- Re-keying numbers every quarter

Those actions create a **digital submission.** They do not create **digital records.**

Under Making Tax Digital, HMRC expects data to move from source to submission without manual re-entry. This is what HMRC calls *digital links.*

What HMRC Means by "Digital Links"

A digital link is simply:

> ***A transfer of data that does not involve copying, pasting, or retyping.***

That's it. Examples of digital links include:

- A bank feed pulling transactions into software
- A receipt capture app feeding data into your records

- An invoice raised inside accounting software

Typing totals into a box is not a digital link. This is why spreadsheet-based systems become fragile very quickly. They rely on humans behaving perfectly, every time. HMRC designs systems on the assumption that humans do not do that.

Receipts Are Part of the Record, Not an Optional Extra

Under Self Assessment, receipts mostly existed as evidence. You only needed them if HMRC asked.

Under Making Tax Digital, receipts become part of the process, even if HMRC never looks at them. The expectation is that:

- The transaction is recorded digitally
- The data supporting it is captured digitally
- Supporting evidence is retained in a digital form

That evidence does not have to be a scanned receipt attached to every transaction. But it does need to exist digitally and be easily linked to the record if HMRC asks.

A faded paper slip in a drawer is not a digital record. A photo stored inside accounting software, or in a connected digital system, is. This is not about HMRC checking every receipt. It's about making sure your records already exist if they ever need to be checked.

The Shoebox Problem

The shoebox approach worked because everything

happened once a year. Making Tax Digital breaks that model. Quarterly reporting means:

- Receipts need to be captured continuously
- Gaps become visible quickly
- Errors repeat four times instead of once

People who leave everything to the end are not just late. They are structurally non-compliant. That is why MTD feels oppressive to some people. It forces behaviour change.

The System HMRC Actually Expects

If you strip away the jargon, HMRC expects this:

- Money comes in or goes out
- The transaction is recorded digitally
- Supporting evidence is retained digitally
- The data flows into a quarterly update

That's it.

Most people choose to attach receipts inside their accounting software because it is the simplest way to meet that expectation. Not because HMRC demands it, but because it removes doubt later.

Modern tools can scan a receipt, extract the data using machine learning, and feed it straight into your accounting software. What once took minutes of manual processing now happens almost instantly.

I'll explain that process later in the book. But see it for what it is: an advantage.

If, like me many years ago, you ever timed how long it

took for someone to manually process a piece of paper into a system, you'll understand why these tools save both time and money.

If your system can do this, you are compliant. If it cannot, you will be fighting it constantly.

But don't panic. I'm going to show you how to implement a system that works.

End-of-Chapter Checklist

✅ I understand the difference between digital records and digital submission

✅ I know what HMRC means by a digital link

✅ I understand why receipts must be captured as part of the process

✅ I can see why annual catch-ups no longer work

6

WHY SPREADSHEETS TECHNICALLY WORK AND PRACTICALLY FAIL

About six months before I started writing this book, I recorded a video on YouTube about Making Tax Digital. It did well. Lots of views. Lots of comments. But one comment lodged itself firmly in my brain:

"You can use spreadsheets!!!!"

Four exclamation marks. Always a good sign.

To be fair, the commenter wasn't wrong. In that video, I was clearly advocating a particular software solution, Xero, and I'll do the same later in this book. Not because I'm on commission, I'm not, but because I've spent years living inside different systems as an accountant and I care deeply about friction.

This chapter will upset the spreadsheet crew. That's deliberate.

It sits immediately after the chapter on digital records and digital links for a reason. Before we go any further, you need to understand a few uncomfortable truths about spreadsheets under Making Tax Digital.

Here's the first one:

Yes, spreadsheets *can* be compliant. And that is exactly the problem.

The Technical Truth

HMRC does not ban spreadsheets. If you:

- Keep accurate digital records
- Maintain valid digital links
- Use compliant bridging software
- Avoid manual re-entry
- Submit correctly every quarter

Then yes, spreadsheets can work. In theory.

The Practical Reality

In practice, spreadsheets fail for five reasons.

Problem 1 – They Rely on Perfect Behaviour

Spreadsheets assume that:

- You never overwrite a formula
- You never paste over a cell
- You never forget to update a tab
- You never change the structure mid-year

That might work in a controlled accounting environment. It does not work for busy business owners and landlords juggling customers, jobs, tenants, and real life.

Problem 2 – They Break Quietly

When accounting software breaks, it usually tells you.

- Bank feeds fail.
- Connections drop.
- Warnings appear

When spreadsheets break, they smile politely and give you the wrong answer. You often don't realise until it's too late.

Problem 3 – Bridging Software Adds Fragility, Not Simplicity

Bridging software exists to connect spreadsheets to HMRC. On paper, it sounds simple. In reality:

- Cells must stay in fixed positions
- Structures cannot change easily
- One small mistake breaks the digital link
- Debugging is stressful and time-consuming

Most people who start with bridging software eventually abandon it. Not because it's illegal. Because it's exhausting.

I saw exactly the same pattern when VAT first moved into Making Tax Digital. Accountancy firms that were comfortable with spreadsheets took clients down the bridging-software route because it felt familiar and safe. In practice, it rarely was.

I can say this from first-hand experience: bridging software looks like a shortcut, but it quickly becomes a maintenance job. Every quarter, structures must stay perfect. Cells can't move. Tabs can't change. One small tweak breaks the digital link and turns a routine submission into a stressful debugging exercise.

Over time, even HMRC has recognised this. Bridging software was tolerated to ease transition, not because it represents a good long-term solution. Everything about the direction of travel suggests this approach will be quietly phased out as native digital systems become the norm.

There's also a more human problem.

Most people using spreadsheet-based systems are not spreadsheet experts. They don't live in formulas, validation rules, or audit trails. So when a spreadsheet breaks, and eventually it will, they don't just lose time. They lose confidence.

> ***And once confidence goes, system avoidance follows.***

That is why spreadsheet solutions tend to fail under Making Tax Digital. Not because people are incapable, but because the system demands a level of precision and discipline that spreadsheets quietly punish.

Problem 4 – Quarterly Pressure Changes Behaviour

Under annual reporting, a spreadsheet could limp along. Under quarterly reporting:

- Errors compound
- Fixes repeat
- Stress increases fourfold

What felt manageable once a year becomes intolerable every three months.

Problem 5 – Spreadsheets Do Not Change Habits

Making Tax Digital is a habits problem, not a software problem. Spreadsheets allow people to:

- Delay
- Batch
- Avoid engagement

MTD punishes all three. Proper accounting software, used correctly, forces regular interaction. That feels uncomfortable at first. Long term, it is calming.

We saw this clearly when VAT moved into Making Tax Digital. In the early days, software solutions were still finding their feet. Bank feeds were patchy. Interfaces were clunky. Trust was low. That was nearly a decade ago.

Since then, there have been years of development, debugging, and real-world use. The good software has improved dramatically. The bad ideas have quietly disappeared. What's left now are systems that are far more stable, intuitive, and forgiving than people expect.

The discomfort most people feel today is not about immature technology. It's about changing habits. Once those habits settle, the software stops feeling intrusive and starts feeling supportive. And that is when MTD stops being something you deal with and becomes something that simply runs in the background.

The Honest Conclusion

People cling to spreadsheets for predictable reasons. They feel cheap. They feel familiar. And if you've survived with them before, they create a false sense of competence. None of those reasons age well under Making Tax Digital.

Specialist accounting software is no longer expensive or exotic. For most people, it costs less than an hour of time a month. Even at living wage, that hour is worth more than the subscription. And unlike spreadsheets, software does not rely on memory, discipline, or perfect behaviour to keep working.

I say this as someone who has spent over twenty years running businesses and building systems. I've lived before this software existed, and I've seen what happens after it's adopted properly. The difference isn't technical. It's psychological. Stress drops. Visibility improves.Decisions get easier. Yes, spreadsheets are legally possible. But they are fragile, unforgiving, and badly matched to how humans actually work.

That is why people who prepare properly for Making Tax Digital almost always move away from them. Not because HMRC forces the issue, but because once better systems are in place, going back simply doesn't make sense. Life is easier when your systems work with you, not against you.

End-of-Chapter Checklist

✅ I understand why spreadsheets are risky under quarterly reporting

✅ I know what bridging software actually involves

✅ I can see how errors compound under MTD

✅ I am thinking about systems, not just compliance

PART 3. LET'S BUILD A SYSTEM THAT WORKS

7

WHAT A COMPLIANT MTD SYSTEM MUST DO

You've made it to Part 3 of the book, and in my opinion this is the most important section.

The first two parts were necessary. I needed to convince you that Making Tax Digital is happening, explain when and how it applies, and clear away the confusion around terminology. If you only read those sections, you'd already be better prepared than about 90% of people affected by MTD.

But this is where things actually get easier. This part of the book is about building a system that works.

There's a bit of business development thinking in here. I've taught innovation at a local university, and I've seen first-hand how good process design can transform large organisations like the NHS and police forces. The scale doesn't matter. Whether it's a national organisation or a one-person business, getting the system right is powerful.

~

Before we go any further, I need to make one thing clear:

Making Tax Digital is not asking you to become better at tax. It is asking you to build a system that behaves predictably.

The good news is this: you've almost certainly already done this elsewhere in your business.

One of my clients is a specialist heating engineer called Shaun. Early on, he said to me,

"I don't think I can systemise my business. What I do is too specialised."

So I asked him a simple question.

"Can you talk me through the steps involved in servicing a standard gas boiler?"

"Yes," he said, without hesitation.

That was the moment it clicked.

Shaun was thinking about his business only in terms of complex heating systems. But like every business, there were plenty of areas that weren't specialised at all: answering the phone, surveying a property with an iPad, taking measurements, managing quotes, following up customers, dealing with paperwork, using software.

Each of those things already had a process.

Accountancy sits firmly in that category.

What this chapter does is show you how to uncover those steps, simplify them, and turn them into a system that runs quietly in the background.

That's the magic.

Start With the System, Not the Software

Most people start in the wrong place.

They are sitting on the sofa in the evening, half watching

television, when an advert for some "MTD compliant" software appears. The advert does its job. It talks about receipt scanning, mobile apps, AI, automation.

STOP.

A well placed advert has just removed your ability to think clearly. You sign up for a free trial and feel productive. You are "doing something".

Software is a secondary decision.

A system exists whether you design one or not and if you don't design it deliberately, you end up with one built from ad hoc decisions, manual work, and stress at deadlines.

So let's define the system first.

How your business actually works

We need to think about what is really going on in your business. Money flows through a business like this:

Inputs → System → Delivery → Outcomes → Money

- **Inputs** - Sales enquiries, staff time, materials, tools, energy, knowledge. These are the raw ingredients.
- **System** - How your business turns inputs into something sellable. Your workflows, processes, habits, and software.
- **Delivery** - The product or service your customer receives.
- **Outcomes** - Customer satisfaction, referrals, repeat work, and learning that improves efficiency.
- **Money** - Profit, cash flow, and business value. Money is not the outcome you manage first. It is

the reflection of everything that happened earlier.

Money is the last stage in the system.

What you are really designing is an accounting system that captures money as each stage happens.

For example, I use proposal software that links to my accounting software. When someone signs, the sales invoice is created automatically. It even prompts the client to set up a Direct Debit. That means while I am still at the "inputs" stage, I am already designing how money will be handled later. When cash hits the bank, it is easy to match and most of the admin is already done.

Your own system does not need to be as advanced as my setup. Many accounting systems include a quoting feature where a client can accept with one click, and the same data automatically becomes your invoice. The system does the boring work for you but the key is thinking about what will actually be useful within your chosen accounting software *before* you buy it.

So when you see that advert, stop. Think about the flow first:

Inputs → System → Delivery → Outcomes → Money

That flow should drive your software choice, not the other way round.

A while ago, an ice cream manufacturer and wholesaler with retail operations asked me to redesign their entire financial setup and modernise it. They were asking me to take a sledgehammer to what they had and rebuild it so it worked like an orchestra.

You only do that if you are confident you can put the

engine back together again. I can, because I follow the same process every time.

Now we can design an MTD compliant system that fits how your business actually works.

The Four Parts of a Compliant MTD System

We are now ready to start designing your own compliant Making Tax Digital system. It has four parts. If you get each part right before rushing into software choice, you will be streets ahead of most people. So what are they?

- **Inputs**
- **Processing**
- **Outputs**
- **Review**

In my book *The Science of Business* I talked about turning data into information, then using that information to make calm decisions. MTD is the same. It is not about being good at tax. It is about building a system that produces clean data, consistently, without heroics.

If one of these four parts is weak, the whole thing starts to wobble. And when it wobbles, humans do what humans always do. They delay, they avoid, they batch, they panic.

So let's design the system to work with humans, not against them.

1. Inputs - Where Data Comes From and bank feeds

Inputs are simply the moments money enters or leaves your world.

For most sole traders and landlords, inputs are:

- bank transactions
- invoices raised
- receipts and bills

A compliant system must:

- capture inputs digitally
- capture them as they happen
- avoid manual re-entry

This is why bank feeds matter. A bank feed is a secure connection that automatically pulls your bank transactions into your accounting software. It's one of the most important decisions you're about to make, and getting a good feed means solid uptime and fewer headaches.

Bank feeds remove memory, guesswork, and transcription errors. More importantly, they remove the need for you to "catch up" later. A bank feed makes transactions appear, almost by magic, already sitting in your bookkeeping software.

If a transaction does not appear digitally at source, the system is fragile from the start. Everything downstream becomes harder.

So how do you choose the right bank?

Bank Choice and Account Conduct

The first question isn't, does your bank support bank feeds, but how good are they and are they free?

Some personal accounts don't offer bank feeds at all. The banks simply aren't set up for it. I helped a portfolio landlord recently who was using different bank accounts to manage different properties. In truth, this sort of tracing by property can be done away with once you adopt software.

In this case, the first bank feed was included, but to access additional feeds he had to pay.

The more modern online banks tend to have excellent bank feeds, although some operate on paid subscription models. These are players like Starling, Monzo, and Tide. One of these was where I ran into issues with that client. These banks integrate via their own banking apps rather than directly inside the accounting software. Because they're relatively new to the market, they've been able to build modern technology from the ground up. As a techie, I know this is what's called a direct API integration.

Some of the high-street banks: Barclays, Lloyds, HSBC and the rest use a different type of connection. Typically, you click a link inside the accounting software and connect from there. Historically, these feeds were more problematic and often needed renewing every three months.

That said, these connections have improved significantly. Renewals now take seconds. Occasionally a transaction might be missed, which is why your accountant should always be checking the software balance against the actual bank statement. Because these feeds have been bolted onto older internet banking systems, they're not always as robust but having said that, I've used a high-street bank feed myself for years without too many issues. If you're happy with your bank, don't move purely for the sake of it.

There is still at least one high-street bank which I won't name but requires you to print and post a form to set up a bank feed. So do ask questions before committing.

I'm not going to direct you to any specific bank. There are many reasons you might need a high-street bank rather than an online one, including access to funding or in-person support.

Personal vs business accounts

One of my landlord clients had been using HSBC personal accounts for years to manage their portfolio. When we integrated the bank feed, it worked reasonably well. But there's no proper management area within HSBC's personal online banking. Because they'd previously connected to another software provider, we had issues removing the old connection.

I've used HSBC business banking for years and have full control over the feeds. The reality is that personal banking platforms aren't designed for running a business and in many cases, it's probably against the terms and conditions.

As a landlord, I've managed properties through personal accounts myself without too much difficulty. But for a sole trader, I would always recommend opening a business account. We saw real problems during COVID where people struggled to access support payments because they didn't have proper business banking in place.

You can probably see now why bank feeds are such a key part of the MTD story. They remove memory, guesswork, and transcription errors. And more importantly, they remove the need to "catch up" later.

Account conduct matters

All HMRC-approved MTD software supports bank feeds, so the real question becomes this:

How organised are your bank accounts? Do you have good account conduct?

One of my clients, a plasterer, doesn't have a separate business bank account. That means his weekly shop, pints down the pub, clothes shopping, and daily pit stop at Greggs (we are in the North East) all get imported into the accounting software. We then end up hunting for supplier and customer payments. God forbid he buys something personal from the same place he buys materials.

That mate who's left a funny reference on the bank line or the purchase of some very personal underwear, it all gets imported too. I've met plenty of HMRC inspectors over the years and they're professionals, but leaving thousands of unrelated transactions in your accounting records causes problems and it makes inspections more challenging.

Remember, everything has to be reconciled and allocated, usually to drawings, it's a complete waste of time, and time is money. Second, it's a source of mistakes. Third, it makes it difficult to analyse things later.

I think you get the idea. Don't do it. Open a separate bank account for your business and keep it strictly for that purpose.

2. Processing: Turning Data Into Information

A bank feed is now doing the heavy lifting, quietly moving your data into your bookkeeping system.

The next job is to think about what happens to that data once it arrives. Specifically, how:

- transactions are categorised
- receipts are linked
- income is matched to invoices

Every piece of bookkeeping software has a different

feature list and price point. That isn't the decision. The real question is how your business actually operates. Get that right and the software choice usually becomes obvious.

One system might be £5 a month cheaper than another. Don't go down that rabbit hole. £5 a month is irrelevant if the software saves you an hour of your time. Time is the scarce resource, not subscription fees.

When processing data becomes easy, something interesting happens. You stop firefighting and start noticing opportunities. A wish list appears, not because you suddenly want bells and whistles, but because the basics are finally under control.

If you're a marketing consultant or work in the trades, producing quotes and invoices is non-negotiable. Under Making Tax Digital, invoices should be raised inside your bookkeeping software, not in third-party tools like Word. That might sound like a chore. It isn't.

I have a freelance video editor client who recently moved onto accounting software. I showed her how to send a quote from the system. The client could click a button to accept it, and the software automatically generated the sales invoice from the same information. That single click saved around ten minutes for every accepted quote.

This is what I mean by *busy fools*. We do extra work out of habit, not because it adds value. Software removes friction when we let it.

Once software starts doing its job properly, it becomes genuinely useful. You get a clear list of who owes you money and for how long. Clients can pay online by card or direct debit. With a couple of clicks, you can send statements or integrate specialist chasing tools for slow payers.

For that same video editing client, something else happened. They now had an organised list of outstanding quotes to follow up at the start of each week. Data collection wasn't forced, it happened naturally.

Most owner-run businesses are badly organised. That's not a criticism; it's reality. A client recently told me they needed more sales. I asked three simple questions:

- Do you follow up on quotes?
- Do you have an organised list of clients?
- Do you send information to clients about how to get the best from your service?

The answer to all three was no. They were relying entirely on the phone ringing. That is a huge missed opportunity.

Moving onto proper accounting software can do far more for a small business than people realise. MTD may be something you *have* to do, but many of the behaviours it nudges you towards are genuinely positive.

Good processing is boring and that's a compliment. Consistency and predictability are what turn MTD compliance into something that quietly runs in the background.

Why reconciliation keeps you in control

Reconciliation is the process of checking that what the software thinks happened in the bank matches what actually happened in the bank. With a bank feed, the software pulls in real transactions and you simply confirm which invoice, bill, or expense each one relates to. Once reconciled, you know the numbers are accurate and nothing is missing or duplicated.

A bank feed brings transactions in automatically, but you still need to perform a processing step to decide where they go in your accounts. Reconciliation is the moment you ask one simple question:

> ***"Do these records actually match what happened in the bank?"***

Reconciliation is simple in concept but comes with a few important complexities. We need to ensure that:

- every transaction in your bank account appears in the software
- nothing is duplicated
- nothing is missing
- the balance in the software agrees with the real bank balance

This is why I've spent so much time talking about bank feed choice. Good feeds prevent duplication and missing transactions, which means the software balance actually agrees to the bank.

I've taken over countless sets of accounts from other accountancy firms. In around 25% of cases, the bank balance is wrong and it's treated as "not a big deal". It *is* a big deal. Unless we first verify that the number is right, we can never know whether anything built on top of it is right. I'll come back to this point in the next chapter.

I was once doing some advanced bookkeeping training with a brilliant financial controller called Bethany. She wasn't formally trained as a bookkeeper but had a natural talent for accounts. It had been two weeks since I'd last seen her, and I'd left her with a process. The very first step on that list said:

"Ensure the bank balance in the accounting software matches the bank balance."

The first thing I checked was the bank balance. It was wrong.

I asked her, "Why didn't you call me?"

"It was only out by £12.45, so I didn't want to bother you."

It turned out the bank had a system failure over a long weekend and the bank feed hadn't worked. We were missing around £40,000 of incoming transactions and £40,000 of outgoing transactions. That's £80,000 of transactions missing. Oops.

The key takeaway is simple: the statement balance is critical. In our firm, if that number is wrong, it becomes a mission-critical issue and goes straight to the top of the list.

Why this matters under Making Tax Digital is straightforward. HMRC assumes your numbers are grounded in reconciled data. If reconciliation is weak, everything built on top of it is guesswork.

Reconciliation Is the Moment of Truth

People hear "bank reconciliation" and imagine something technical or fiddly. In modern software, it isn't. You see the transaction, confirm what it is, and move on.

When reconciliation works properly, errors are spotted early, mistakes don't repeat for months, and confidence replaces avoidance. When it doesn't, small issues compound, quarterly updates feel stressful, and people stop trusting their own numbers. That loss of trust is where panic starts.

Reconciliation doesn't reward tax knowledge; it rewards regular attention. You're not "doing accounts" you're sanity-checking reality. That's why it fits perfectly with the 15-minute weekly habit system I've produced for you later in the book.

A reconciled system means the numbers are believable. Cash flow conversations are grounded, and quarterly updates become a by-product, not a project.

If the software balance matches the bank, you can relax. If it doesn't, something needs attention and the sooner you look, the cheaper it is to fix.

Automation Is Not a Luxury

When I say automation, I do not mean clever. I mean stable. Automation is not about sophistication. It is about reducing decisions.

When:

- bank rules learn your spending
- receipt tools extract data
- software remembers suppliers

...you are no longer relying on willpower. You are relying on a system.

That is what gets you through busy periods, holidays, illness, and the weeks where everything is going wrong. So this is an essential consideration when choosing a software solutions and building your system.

3. Outputs: What Leaves the System

Outputs are what the system produces. This is where, as an entrepreneur and landlord, I start to get excited. This is the stage where I get to see my profit and loss, my cash flow, and what all the activity actually means.

We're calling this Stage 3: outputs — although I nearly

labelled it Stage 4, because the output stage actually happens twice.

Why?

Because the first output is really a review of accuracy and a search for adjustments. The second output is what happens once everything has been corrected.

You might find no errors. Bah! Look closer. Even with all my years of experience, if I'm processing hundreds of transactions, a mistake will always creep in and that's before I've even considered any more advanced adjustments.

Under Making Tax Digital, outputs include:

- quarterly updates to HMRC
- the year-end final declaration
- reports for you

Here's the key idea:

> ***Outputs should be a consequence, not an effort. Most importantly, we must check accuracy before anything is submitted to HMRC.***

In a good system:

- the data is already there
- the numbers already make sense
- submission is a review, not a rebuild

That's the difference between *"quarterly reporting is stressful"* and *"quarterly reporting is uneventful"*. As all we should be doing is a few checks.

. . .

So how do I review things?

It's tempting to rush straight into running a profit and loss report, but the first questions I ask are:

- Does the bank balance in the software match the actual bank balance? (Remember I mentioned this earlier.)
- Are all bank lines reconciled on all bank accounts?
- If I'm using receipt capture software, have we added everything?
- Do I agree with the outstanding customer and supplier invoices?

Only at that stage do I start running reports.

I begin with a profit and loss report showing four months of comparatives in columns, with a fifth column for year-to-date figures. I've found that four months is ideal, because quarterly-paid items can be missed if you only look at three months. At this point, I'm looking for patterns I can explain and understand.

For example, a £50-a-month software subscription should be steady each month. If I see that it's jumped to £100 in one month, I'll ask why and investigate. That could be a mistake, or it could highlight an action that improves the business. For example, spotting a forgotten auto-renewal that needs cancelling.

The year-to-date column gives me a rough sense of what my tax bill is shaping up to look like at the year end.

Once I'm happy with the profit and loss, I'll check the balance sheet. While around 95% of my clients understand the P&L, only about 5% can extract real management insight from the balance sheet, and most sole traders and landlords under MTD won't find it especially useful. My advice is this: if you do the basics I've outlined here and skip a detailed balance sheet review, you're already streets ahead of most people.

One report I always look at is the statement of cash flows in the software. It shows me where the money has actually gone. Simple checks like reviewing customer invoices each quarter can highlight late payers, head off bad debts, and help you understand cash flow.

So while MTD operates on a quarterly cycle, I review my financial reports: profit and loss, balance sheet, and cash flow; every month.

"Justin, why are you doing this extra work?"

Because last month I wanted to understand why I had £37,000 of late customer payments, rather than waiting three months to discover it had grown to £45,000. That's a big cash hole to fill.

That's why it's worth looking at the reports. The real value isn't MTD compliance, it's running your business better.

4. Review: The Missing Piece

One of my clients, Matt, once said to me,

"Justin, I love working with your firm because you're not archaeologists."

"Excuse me, you're going to have to explain that."

"Every accountant I've worked with before is digging through transactions from six months ago. It's all too late. The way you've designed the systems in our business gives us real-time financial accounts on tap. We're waiting days for accurate reports after month end, not months. We're having conversations about changes while there's still time for them to make a difference."

Review is the part most people skip. A simple review asks:

- does this look right?
- are there any obvious gaps?
- has anything unusual happened?

This isn't deep analysis. It's pattern recognition.

That's why having a simple, written bookkeeping process matters. For example, does a software licence go to IT and software costs, or to subscriptions? That might sound picky, but when you're comparing patterns over time, it matters and during reviews it becomes frustrating if it's inconsistent.

When I produce management accounts for venture capital firms, they get irritated very quickly by these inconsistencies. How can someone unfamiliar with your accounts compare anything? Now, for a moment, swap that VC for an HMRC inspector. You get the idea.

Earlier, I talked about the concept of two outputs. Review is what happens in that first output. We're making sure everything is right before we hand documents over to HMRC or investors.

Ten minutes of review can catch problems that would take hours to fix later. It also means we have management information we can actually use to decide our next business move. And that's where the real win sits;not compliance, but control.

The Secret

Our rep from Dext, Amina, shows me our stats each quarter. We process around 15,000 documents every three months. She told me that roughly 29% were being processed automatically, with no human input.

It immediately became my mission to increase that by just 6%. That's 3,600 extra documents per year processed without anyone touching them.

Here's the secret: that improvement doesn't happen in processing, it happens in review.

When you spot a mistake, you fix it in a way that stops it happening again. You talk to your bookkeepers and optimise the automation. This overlaps slightly with processing, but it really belongs in review, because this is where we hold up a mirror and ask, *"Can we make this more efficient?"*

My long-suffering team roll their eyes when I say,

"I've worked out that we do this task 1,000 times a month. I've timed how long it takes and I've got an idea to make it better..."

The Minimum Viable MTD System

A compliant MTD system does not need to be impressive.

At a minimum, it needs:

- a separate bank account
- accounting software with MTD capability
- a weekly or fortnightly review habit

That is enough. Anything more is optimisation. Anything less creates friction.

I'm going to look at specific processes to help you with your bookkeeping later in the book. You may notice that I haven't gone into detail on receipt capture and scanning at this stage. That's deliberate. It doesn't apply to every business, and it's far more useful once the wider system is clear. I'll address it properly in the next chapter.

End-of-Chapter Checklist

- ✅ I understand the system
- ✅ I know where problems really start
- ✅ I see why automation matters
- ✅ I understand why review keeps me compliant

8

SOFTWARE SOLUTIONS

I was in the pub with some friends last night. Their son was there too, just about to head off to university and trying to decide between different flavours of computer science.

Within minutes, I found myself talking about Replit, an AI-powered code-writing tool I've been playing with. How I'd used it to knock together a small web app, and how GitHub repositories can now be wired into AI tools so they can help debug your code.

At this point, my friends were looking at me with a mix of confusion and regret. Clearly wondering why they'd invited me out in the first place. Given that my day job is primarily running an accountancy firm, not writing software.

The ice was finally broken when someone said, "Geek!" Actually, I think it was my wife. Everyone laughed.

The reason I tell you that story is this. While I'm no longer a professional developer, I still spend a lot of time messing about with technology. Code, automation, and AI.

Not because it's my job, but because I want to be one of the best systems accountants in the UK.

You cannot do that without understanding how good technology behaves, and just as importantly, how bad technology behaves. This book was born out of my desire to properly understand Making Tax Digital, not just the rules, but the systems behind it.

That doesn't mean I chase shiny tools or believe there's one perfect setup. Quite the opposite. I'm a fairly ruthless judge of what's useful and what's not. I have to live inside these systems every day, running businesses, supporting clients, and fixing things when they go wrong.

I also want to make something very clear before we go any further:

There is no single technology setup that's right for everyone.

In this chapter, I'm going to walk you through some of the choices I've made and the tools I use. Keep the last chapter firmly in mind. Software only works when it supports a well-designed system.

It cannot fix a broken one, and the needs of your business should dictate the software you choose.

What software do I use?

I've used most accounting software over the years, but I'm going to advocate for Xero. Why?

Because I actually have to live inside these systems while running businesses and supporting clients. Let me explain.

There's a well-known name in the accountancy software market that's been trying to catch up in recent years. Their name reminds me of a herb, but I won't say which one.

We had a tax return client using their software. I saw one of my colleagues logged in and asked how he was finding it.

His response came with some anger.

"You can only compare two years on the balance sheet. I'm trying to track down a problem and I've had to use a cutting tool. When you download a report it disappears into a little box in the top-right corner. It takes five clicks to get a simple download. Some figures are clickable, others aren't. It's just painful."

His conclusion was short and clear: "It's crap."

And it's not just that provider.

There's another very well-known platform with a huge advertising budget. On paper it looks impressive. In reality, the user interface just isn't good enough. Any report that needs a sideways scroll bar goes straight to the bottom of my list.

My point is this: I've tried them all.

So this chapter isn't about brand loyalty. This is why I advocate for Xero. No, I'm not paid to do so. I use it because, in practice, it's the best solution I've found. Plus I saw a working MTD submission system in early summer 2025 well before I started writing this book.

> **This chapter is about friction. I do*n't do friction!***

Software systems have to work quickly and predictably, or people stop using them properly.

Making Tax Digital changes the rhythm of tax. It moves

people from once-a-year panic to regular, predictable habits. And when that happens, weak systems become your worst nightmare.

That's why I keep coming back to Xero. Not because it's perfect but because it reduces friction and supports routine. And routine is what keeps you compliant when life gets busy.

You might see another piece of software in the market and say it has features Xero doesn't have. If that other software will reduce friction in your world then it could be right for you.

Software and Accountants

I think a large proportion of people will still need help from an accountant. In fact, I think it is madness that more people do not use one. In many cases, a decent accountant will save more in missed reliefs and simple tax planning than their fee costs. Nothing clever. Just applying the rules properly.

Doing a tax return is not difficult. What makes it hard is poor information. I have completed thousands of Self Assessment returns. The difference between a smooth job and a painful one is not tax complexity. It is how organised the records are.

Let me give you two real-world examples.

One client sent over their records as a pile of bank statements with no explanation. Each statement arrived in a separate email. Twelve emails. No context. No notes. This was ten days before the deadline. Their tax affairs were relatively simple, but we were battling from the first minute. We spent time reconstructing what had happened instead of applying tax knowledge. The work was harder, slower, and more stressful for everyone involved.

Another client emailed eight months before the deadline to say, "My year-end bookkeeping is done in Xero. I have a couple of questions about how I've coded some expenses." That is perfect. Now I can do what an accountant is meant to do. I can review categories properly. I can ask sensible questions. "Should we consider home use or the basis of travel calculations?" "Have we claimed all the CIS suffered?"

The value in that second example is obvious. The information is already organised and it arrived early, so my skill is used on tax decisions, not detective work. It also lets us move into the next level of work, often referred to as "advisory". This is simply pointing out practical ways the business can improve, rather than just reporting what has already happened.

The first client was firefighting. The second had a system. One is MTD-ready. The other is not. Last-minute working leaves no time for advice and leads to surprise tax bills. In that situation, you are not paying for an accountant. You are paying for an emergency admin assistant.

This is why software choice is not just about you.

For years, when a company client came to us, we were clear. We only support Xero. If you do not want to use Xero, we are probably not the right firm for you. In reality, this was rarely an issue. The reason for that policy comes from my background in software development. Supporting too many platforms means you become average at all of them. No one in the team develops real depth. At Orange

Umbrella, every team member is Xero-certified and refreshes that training each year. When a client asks for help, they get an answer. Not a shrug.

When Making Tax Digital for VAT first came in, many firms made what I think was a mistake. They told clients, "You need MTD software," and then either let clients choose or offered a couple of options. Clients were set up and left to get on with it. When problems appeared, the firm could not support the system properly. That is how software becomes a burden instead of an enabler.

As we move into quarterly reporting for income tax, this matters even more. Choosing an accountant is no longer just about technical tax skill. It is also about whether their systems match yours. If you use software your accountant does not understand well, friction appears immediately. Their processes will not fit your setup. The support will feel clumsy. The experience will be worse for both sides.

So when you choose an accountant, ask about software. Ask what they support properly. Ask how they work with it in practice. This is not about brand loyalty. It is about whether their system and your system are compatible.

The final chapter of this book goes deeper into whether you need an accountant at all. I wanted to include this here because technology choice and professional support are now tied together. You cannot separate them anymore.

I do feel some sympathy for accountants. The job is changing. You are now expected to be a technologist and an accountant. That shift is uncomfortable. But it is also unavoidable. Making Tax Digital does not just change reporting. It changes what "good professional support" looks like.

If I found a brilliant accountant I genuinely trusted, but they only supported QuickBooks, I would stick with that accountant. Trust matters more than tools. We see the best and worst moments of people's businesses, and often their personal lives too. That level of access only works when there is trust. I would rather sacrifice software features than lose the person I trust at my side.

How I Judge Accounting Software

I don't choose accounting software based on feature lists. I judge it by how it behaves when I'm actually using it. How quickly can I see what's going on? How many clicks does everyday work take? Can I drill into numbers without friction? Does the layout help me think clearly, or does it get in the way?

If software fails these tests, it does not last long in my world. Good accounting is not about having more features. It is about a simple loop that runs smoothly. Data goes in. You review it. You spot something odd. You fix it. Then you move on. Software either supports that loop or quietly trains you to avoid it. There is no middle ground.

Why Speed and Layout Matter Under Making Tax Digital

Making Tax Digital means you will look at your numbers more often. When frequency goes up, speed starts to matter. If reports are slow to open, you stop opening them. If comparisons take too many steps, you stop checking. If drilling into detail feels awkward, you stop trusting what you are seeing. When people stop looking, small errors grow quietly in the background.

Layout matters for the same reason. If reports are cramped, sideways, or tiring to read, your brain has to work harder than it should. My experience with Xero is that reports are readable. Drill-down feels natural. Common tasks do not feel like work.

Top Tip

At this point in the book, you might be thinking, "Is he right about Xero?" That's healthy scepticism.

One warning though. If you choose your software based on the last advert you saw on TV, you are effectively committing to a long term relationship. Switching later is possible, but it is painful.

At the time of writing, there are three big players in this space: Sage, QuickBooks, and Xero. All three offer free trials. Use the trials properly.

A proper test means:

- Doing the initial setup
- Connecting the bank feed
- Reconciling some transactions
- Raising an invoice
- Running a few basic reports

Do not just judge how it looks. Judge how fast and natural common tasks feel. Speed and flow matter as much as features.

Correction Speed Is Non-Negotiable

Quarterly reporting changes one thing more than any other. Mistakes have to be easy to fix. You need to be able to recode errors quickly, work through transactions in bulk, and spot patterns early enough to correct them before they repeat. In Xero, for example, I can use the "Find and

Recode" feature to fix a batch of mis-coded transactions in seconds instead of clicking through them one by one. That matters. If fixing mistakes feels painful, people delay it. Delays turn small problems into big ones.

This is why I care so much about bank feeds and reconciliation screens. A good reconciliation workflow is not a nice extra. It is how you stay in control of the system.

Getting going with Software

This is the bit most people miss. Software is not the system, it is just one part of it. The real question is whether information flows cleanly from real life into your accounts. If it does, Making Tax Digital feels calm. If it does not, MTD feels chaotic. That is what I mean by systems accountancy. Not "which app is best", but where data starts, where it ends, and what breaks in between.

Xero fits well here because it supports bank feeds, integrated receipt capture via Hubdoc, and efficient reconciliation. If you want a more advanced receipt capture tool, something like Dext can sit on top, but it is an upgrade, not a requirement. I will come on to connected apps in a moment.

Which Version

This is where people often overspend. Most sole traders and landlords *do not* need advanced analytics, complex add-ons, or feature-heavy plans that are designed for larger businesses. What you actually need is:

- Bank feeds
- Reliable receipt capture

- Clean reports
- A straightforward route to Making Tax Digital
- Easy correction workflows

The right question isn't "What's the best plan?" It's:

> ***What's the least complex plan that supports good habits?***

That's why it's worth looking at pricing plans carefully. All major accounting platforms have tiers, but in most cases the lowest cost plan will cover what you actually use each week.

For example, Xero has introduced **Xero Simple**. It sits further down the pricing page, so scroll past the main plans to find it. It is a streamlined plan designed for sole traders and landlords. It includes the essentials you need for Making Tax Digital record keeping:

- Bank feeds
- Automatic reconciliation
- Simple invoicing
- Basic reporting

It is also cheaper each month than the broader business editions.

Rather than buying the most expensive plan because it looks powerful on paper, choose the plan that lets you *do the daily, weekly and quarterly work without friction*. The easier it is to keep your records tidy and up to date, the more MTD becomes a background habit and less of a stress.

. . .

Tracking Categories and Nominal Structure (Design Before Detail)

Once you have chosen the software that is right for you, pause before you start reconciling. There are a couple of design choices to think about first.

Accounting software lets you analyse your business in two main ways.

One is through tracking categories or cost centres.The other is through your nominal structure, sometimes called the chart of accounts.

A quick translation if you are not an accountant:

Nominal codes are just the buckets your income and costs fall into. Travel, fuel, repairs, rent, software, marketing. The chart of accounts is simply the list of those buckets (nominal codes).

Both tools are useful. But they are not equal, and they are not for the same stage of maturity.

Tracking categories are powerful, but they are also easy to misuse. I've given a landlord-specific example of tracking categories by property later in the book, because that is one of the rare cases where they are genuinely transformative. For most people starting out, I would actively discourage setting up tracking categories too early.

They require careful thought. They add complexity. And once you start using them, they shape how data flows through your system.

For well-diversified businesses, they can be brilliant. A logistics company might track profit by region. A fleet operator might track costs by van or truck. A multi-site business might track each location. In those cases, tracking categories help answer real questions that matter.

For most sole traders, I would be surprised if that level of detail ever gets used properly. The data might be there, but if it is never reviewed, it is just extra work.

Where most small businesses get far more value is in nominal structure design.

This is the unglamorous bit of systems design, but it is where clarity is built. If your income and costs are thrown into vague buckets, your reports will always be vague. If they are separated in a way that reflects how your business actually works, your reports become useful.

A simple example

A café might want to separate food sales from drink sales. Not because HMRC cares, but because the owner does. Margins are different. Stock behaves differently. Problems show up in different places. That separation turns reports into decision-making tools.

In my own business, we sell software licences for Xero and Dext. We also pay for those licences ourselves. So we have a clear income line for software licences sold and a corresponding cost of goods sold for software licences purchased. That allows me to see, every month, whether our £4,000 software bill is being covered by licence income. When I review our management accounts, that one line tells me a lot about margin discipline. It is boring but is powerful.

Nominal design does not need to be complex. It just needs to reflect reality.

Xero comes with generic categories like "motor expenses". For one client, Sarah, that was not useful enough. She wanted to see fuel separately from repairs, because fuel was creeping up and she suspected waste. So we renamed "motor expenses" to "Motor – Fuel", added "Motor – Repairs", and then added "Motor – Other" for things like tax and insurance. That small change transformed how useful her reports were. She could now see patterns instead of guessing.

This is the key point. Structure creates meaning. Software just shows you what the structure allows.

This is also where the verification stage becomes valuable. When you review your numbers, you are not just checking for mistakes. You are learning how your business behaves. You are seeing where money actually goes. You are noticing which costs grow quietly and which income lines perform better than expected. That understanding is what turns bookkeeping from admin into management.

Start with a simple nominal structure. Let the system bed in. Add tracking categories later, only if you can clearly explain what question they will help you answer. If you cannot explain the question, you do not need the feature yet.

That is systems accountancy in practice.

Connected Apps: Where Systems Start to Scale

Most people think accounting software is just for recording what has already happened. That mindset keeps businesses small.

The real power of modern bookkeeping systems is not the core software itself. It is what happens when you connect it to the rest of your business.

Xero, like most modern platforms, has an app marketplace. This is where proposal tools, inventory systems, payment platforms, booking systems, and reporting tools plug into your accounting system. The accounting software becomes the centre of gravity. Everything else feeds it clean data.

In my own business, we connect our proposal software to Xero. When a client signs a proposal, it automatically creates their recurring invoice. We raise around 500 invoices a month. Without that connection, someone would be manually creating invoices every month. That is not "admin". That is wasted life.

One of my clients, Gavin, runs a product-based business. We helped him move onto an inventory management system called InFlow and connect it to Xero. Before that, stock was tracked in spreadsheets and memory. Orders were slow. Mistakes were common. After the change, stock levels became visible, reordering became predictable, and fulfilment became smoother. The combination of Xero plus proper inventory software gave him back around two days a week! Not because he worked harder. Because the system stopped fighting him.

This is the part most people underestimate. Connected apps are not just efficiency tools. They are growth tools. They remove bottlenecks. They remove duplication. They allow the business to operate at a scale that would otherwise require more staff, more stress, and more firefighting.

You do not need to design all of this on day one. In fact, you should not. But you should choose accounting software that can grow with you. Xero has a strong ecosystem. So do other platforms. The brand matters less than the availability of integrations that suit how your business actually runs.

The principle is simple. Your accounting software should sit at the centre of your system. Connected apps should reduce manual work, not create more of it. If an app saves you time every single week, it is rarely "too expensive".

The danger is not paying for good tools.The danger is paying in time, mistakes, and stress because you refused to use them.

Opening Accounting Software in the Real World (New vs Existing Businesses)

Opening accounting software is easy if you are starting a brand new business. There is no history. No comparisons. No baggage. You connect the bank feed and move forward.

For existing businesses, this step is often where things quietly go wrong.

When you move onto proper bookkeeping software partway through trading, you are not starting from zero. You are stepping into a story that is already in progress. The numbers you see on day one need to reflect reality. If they do not, nothing you build on top will make sense.

This is where opening balances matter.

Your bank balance on day one in the software must match your real bank balance on that day. Not roughly. Exactly. If it does not, every report that follows will feel wrong. People then blame the software, when the problem is the starting point. We cannot reconcile accurately without an accurate opening bank balance.

The same applies to money owed to you and money you owe.If you have unpaid invoices, they need to exist in the system. If you owe suppliers, those balances need to be there too.

This is not about perfection. It is about continuity.

I see two common mistakes when people move onto proper software.

The first is treating the system as a fresh start and

ignoring the past. The bank feed comes in, but the numbers do not match what they remember. Reports feel wrong from day one, and trust in the system is lost early.

The second is trying to recreate years of history. People drown in detail, burn out, and never reach the point where the system becomes useful.

The right approach sits in the middle.

Get the current position right. Do not try to rebuild your entire financial history. The goal is continuity, not perfection.

This is one of the few points where paying for help at setup is usually worth it. Not forever. Just once.

If the opening position is right, the system starts with credibility. When the numbers feel believable, people use the system. When they do not, people avoid it.

Making Tax Digital amplifies this problem. Quarterly reporting assumes your system is grounded in reality.

If you start from the wrong numbers, you will question every update, every report, and every submission.

One of the easiest points to move onto new software is at the start of a tax year. So, if you are reading this in June, it may be worth setting your system up from April rather than jumping in mid-year. Do not go back further than that.

Do not underestimate setup. If double-entry bookkeeping or trial balances are unfamiliar, getting help at this stage will save you from feeling out of your depth before you even get going.

Receipt Capture

Receipt capture looks like a small detail. In practice, it becomes one of the most important parts of a Making Tax Digital system. MTD does not change the rules on what records you must keep, but it does change how often you have to look at them. When receipts do not enter the system cleanly, everything else becomes harder. Coding slows down. Reconciliation becomes guesswork. Reviews start to feel unreliable. Under quarterly reporting, messy inputs surface more often, so small problems become painful quickly. Most bookkeeping stress does not come from reports. It comes from poor inputs.

There are a few well known tools in this space. The two I know best are Dext and Hubdoc. There are also others in the market, such as AutoEntry. They all aim to solve the same problem, getting real world paperwork into your accounts without manual typing. The differences are not about whether they work at all. They are about how reliably they work when life is busy.

You will also see a lot of talk about "AI" in this area. These tools have been using machine learning for years to read receipts and extract data. Calling it AI is mostly marketing. The label does not matter. What matters is how accurate the extraction is, how easy it is to correct when it gets things wrong, and how quickly the system learns your habits. Do not buy into buzzwords. Pay attention to behaviour. Does it save you time in real life, or does it create more fiddling and checking?

Xero includes basic receipt capture through Hubdoc. For many people, that is enough. If you are starting from nothing, Hubdoc can feel like magic. Take a photo, the receipt appears in your accounts. That alone is a huge upgrade from shoebox accounting. But this is where experience changes your expectations. Once you have used a more advanced tool, it is hard to go back.

We push many clients towards Dext even though it is an extra cost. Not because Hubdoc is bad, but because Dext is built as a premium product. The difference is not subtle once you are inside the workflow. Dext gives you far more control over how suppliers are treated, how data is coded, and how errors are corrected. The interface is faster. The review process is clearer. Over time, those small frictions matter.

One of my clients, Tom, is a good example. He reached the point where his software bill was higher than his accountancy fee and it annoyed him. He cancelled Dext and moved to the receipt capture that came with his Xero licence. Two weeks later, he was back on Dext. This happens more often than you might expect. If you start with the basic tool, you are usually impressed. If you start with the premium tool, going backwards feels painful. It is a bit like doing your food shop at Aldi versus Marks and Spencer. Both will feed you. One just removes more friction.

This is not about brand loyalty. It is about understanding where your system will break under pressure. Receipt capture is the first point of failure for most people. If it is slow, clunky, or unreliable, you will delay using it. Delays turn into batching. Batching turns into missing data. Missing data turns into stress at quarter end.

Volume matters as well.

If you only capture five or ten items a month, paying for a premium tool like Dext is probably pointless. The built in capture in your accounting software will usually be enough.

If you are VAT registered or dealing with hundreds of items a month, a premium product can quickly pay for itself in time saved and fewer errors.

Security Is Part of the System, Not a Feature

Under Making Tax Digital, your accounting system is no longer a standalone piece of software. It connects to your bank, your email, other apps, and HMRC. That means security is now part of system design, not an IT afterthought.

Xero, for example, uses two-factor authentication. That is good practice. But this is the point where most people stop thinking. The real risk is rarely the core software. It is everything connected to it. Your email is often the weakest link. If someone can get into your email, they can reset passwords, approve logins, and intercept invoices. Turning on two-factor authentication on your accounting software but leaving your email unsecured is like fitting a strong front door and leaving the back door open.

The same applies when you start changing how information flows into the system. Many people set up a dedicated email address so suppliers can send invoices directly into Xero or a receipt capture tool. That is efficient. It also creates a new risk point. What controls are in place to spot fake invoices, changed bank details, or simple mistakes? Who reviews what comes in before it is trusted? Automation without review is how fraud and errors slip through quietly.

The moment you start sending sales invoices from your accounting software, there is another quiet technical shift. Your invoices no longer come from your own email server. They come from the software provider's servers. That can affect deliverability and, in rare cases, how professional your emails appear to customers. It is worth speaking to whoever manages your website or email domain about DNS settings and email authentication. This is dull, technical stuff. It is also how you reduce the chance of invoices going to spam or being flagged as suspicious.

The right question is not "is this safe?" It is "where is the weak link?"

Good systems assume that things will fail at some point. They are designed to limit the damage when they do. That mindset applies to security as much as it does to bookkeeping. The larger accounting software providers have put a lot of thought into security within their own platforms. But they cannot manage the risks created by your email, your connected apps, or your internal processes. Those weak links sit outside their control, and that is where most real-world problems arise.

~

The Honest Conclusion

I do not use Xero because it is fashionable. I use it because, in practice, it reduces friction. It supports boring, repeatable habits. It makes review and correction fast enough that people actually do it. When life is busy, that matters more than any feature list.

Making Tax Digital does not reward clever software. It rewards systems that let you think clearly, even when you are tired, rushed, or distracted. If another platform reduces friction better in your world, use that instead. The tool is not the point. The system it supports is.

~

End-of-Chapter Checklist

- ☑ I understand why friction matters under MTD
- ☑ I know what a basic MTD system actually needs

✅ I know the difference between useful features and distracting noise

✅ I know when receipt capture tools add real value

✅ I understand that systems matter more than software choices

SETUP GUIDE

If you decide to use Xero, I've included a QR link below to a simple setup guide that walks you through the basics without overcomplicating things.

PART 4. SOLE TRADERS IN THE REAL WORLD

9

THE REAL WORLD SOLE TRADER

Making Tax Digital does not fail because people are careless. It fails because most real businesses do not behave like neat spreadsheets.

There is also a deep disconnect between how policy is designed and how work actually happens. Many of the people writing government guidance have never had to run a small business in the real world. They assume work happens calmly, at a desk, with time to tidy things up later. That is not how most sole traders operate.

Work happens in vans, on sites, between calls, late at night, and in short bursts between the rest of life. Quarterly reporting exposes this gap. Not because people are bad, but because systems built for "I'll sort it later" collapse under frequency. If you recognise yourself in this chapter, that is not a problem. It means you are about to fix the right thing.

My client Tom is a busy tradesman and thinks the passenger footwell of his van is the in-tray for his receipts. Whether it is a van footwell or a pile on a desk, these systems will cause problems under Making Tax Digital. One day we had a chat and I asked, "Is there someone who can help you?" It turned out his girlfriend was keen to help. She came into the office for some Xero training and off she went. Now Tom puts paper invoices into a poly pocket in the van and his girlfriend scans them into Dext.

I use Tom as an example because his girlfriend did some simple things that made his life easier. She arranged for suppliers to send invoices directly into Dext, the receipt scanning tool. These no longer went to Tom. She also used Dext to analyse supplier statements and spot mistakes.

I am the same as you. Nicola and Dan in my own business ask me every month to add missing receipts. I am usually on top of it, but when I am deep into big projects, like writing a book, it is as if I run out of capacity. That is not a weakness. It is cognitive load. Under pressure, I tend to carry too much myself rather than ask for help. Eventually, even a piece of paper feels like too much. That mindset is almost unfathomable to the civil servant who wrote the guidance.

here will be people reading this who see Making Tax Digital and think, "I'm not sure I can survive this."

That reaction is rarely about tax. It is about overwhelm.

That is why this chapter started with Tom. Before we talk about trades, consultants, creatives, or systems, the first question is simpler:

Do I need help?

Once that question is answered honestly, the next one becomes practical.

What actually pulls me into Making Tax Digital in the first place?

Turnover versus Profit

The first rule that catches most sole traders out under Making Tax Digital is the difference between turnover and profit. This is the distinction that causes the most frustration, and it is also the one HMRC is least interested in debating.

For Making Tax Digital, HMRC looks at turnover, not profit. Turnover is simply the total amount you invoice or receive from your work. It is not what you keep. It is not what you pay yourself. It is not how well the year felt. It is just the top line. Expenses come later. Profit is irrelevant to whether you are pulled into Making Tax Digital. HMRC uses turnover because it is objective and hard to manipulate.

Profit depends on judgement, timing, and how costs are classified. Turnover does not. Making Tax Digital needs a clean entry rule. Turnover provides that. This feels unfair if your business has high costs.

A tradesperson can turn over £60,000 and keep far less than a consultant turning over £40,000 because material costs are higher. That comparison hurts. But HMRC is not measuring success. It is deciding which reporting system you must use. Eligibility and tax payable are two separate conversations.

Once you cross the threshold, you join Making Tax Digital, you submit quarterly updates, and you build compliant systems. Your tax bill may still be modest. Making Tax Digital does not increase tax. It increases visibility. Once you accept that rule, energy spent arguing with it produces nothing. Energy spent designing around it pays dividends.

Top Tips for Sole Traders

We have covered systems design in Chapter 7, but I want to expand on a couple of key points for you as a sole trader.

Tip 1: Separate transactions, not just accounts

I have already argued for using separate bank accounts to avoid mixing personal and business spending. The same thinking applies to receipts. I often pop into Morrisons for a meal deal and, at the same time, pick up soap for the office loo. Some people would put it all through in one go and then debate whether to use the business card or personal card. That is not a dilemma. Just split the transaction. The staff will not bat an eyelid if you put a divider between your shopping. One transaction is personal. One is business. The problem disappears.

Tip 2: Capture the receipt before you drive off

When I get back to the car, before I drive anywhere, out comes my phone and I scan the receipt into Dext. It can then go in the bin and I never have to think about it again. I have a great team who make sure it ends up in the right place in the accounts and reconciles properly. But the critical part of the system is my behaviour at the start. I only need to follow my own process.

Tip 3: Invoice as soon as the work is done

Work always feels more important than admin. That is normal. But the Xero app has been a game changer for many of my clients. If you work on site with customers, change your process so you raise the invoice there and then on the app. Some even ask the customer to pay straight away. One client started doing this and saw an immediate improvement in cash flow. No more late night admin creating invoices in Word. The job is done and the money starts moving sooner.

Under annual reporting, these habits were survivable because memory and year end tidy ups masked the damage. Under quarterly reporting, the gaps show up quickly. The system starts to creak. People then assume Making Tax Digital is the problem. It is not. Weak systems were always there. MTD just removes the ability to ignore them for twelve months at a time.

The fix is rarely complicated. One business account. One business card. One capture habit at the point of spend. No batching. No relying on memory. No end of month archaeology. If money flows through the business account and evidence is captured at source, the system works. If it does not, the system breaks. This is not about being organised. It is about removing the need to be organised. Good systems work when you are tired, rushed, and distracted. That is the design standard to aim for.

Limited Companies

One of my clients said to me,

> ***"I want to incorporate to avoid Making Tax Digital."***

I understand the reaction. Quarterly reporting creates a

natural pause point and makes people step back and question whether their current structure is still right.

It used to be the case that limited companies were almost always more tax efficient. Sometimes that is still true. More often, it is nuanced. In some cases, a company can lead to higher tax bills and more complexity. The tax landscape has changed dramatically over the last decade, and old rules of thumb no longer always apply.

Rushing into a limited company just to avoid MTD is rarely the right answer. It changes your reporting obligations, but it does not automatically improve your tax position. It also creates a long-term structure that can be hard and expensive to unwind.

Do I personally trade as a sole trader? No. I use limited companies because I need to manage risk. A limited company is exactly that, limited. The liability sits with the company, not with you personally.

I sat down with a new client recently and explained that moving to a limited company would likely increase his tax bill. But I also talked him through the risks he was taking as a sole trader. He had third-party suppliers and was working with children. Despite the higher taxes and increased compliance, he chose to incorporate because the risk profile of his work made that the sensible option.

I have always believed that the moment you have other people delivering parts of your service on your behalf, subcontractors, staff, or third-party suppliers dealing with your customers, a limited company deserves serious consideration. In the case above, he had a third-party supplier delivering after-school clubs. Are you really prepared to bet your house on that subcontractor having valid public liability cover?

"It will never happen to me," you might say. A friend of

mine was running a bootcamp business as a sole trader and used another personal trainer to deliver one of his sessions. He checked the insurance cover when they first started working together. It was all fine until someone was injured during a session and lawyers became involved. He was calm at first because he believed the instructor was insured. When he asked for the documents, it turned out the policy had not been renewed. He came close to losing his house. It was one of the most stressful periods of his life. He now trades through a limited company.

There have been recent increases in Companies House fees and changes that mean directors can no longer file their own accounts without commercial software. These are irritations, but they are not good reasons to avoid incorporation if the underlying risk profile of your business points towards limited liability.

If you worked with my accountancy firm and had a limited company, we would put you on almost exactly the same systems as if you were within MTD, Xero, Dext, and the same underlying processes. The systems discipline does not go away just because the reporting regime is different.

A decision to move into a limited company should be taken with proper professional advice. It is not a tax hack. It is a long-term structural decision about risk, liability, and how you want your business to operate.

People who struggle under Making Tax Digital are rarely lazy. They are usually busy, successful, and used to solving problems under pressure. MTD punishes last-minute brilliance. It rewards boring consistency. Once you accept that, the solution becomes obvious. Stop trying to be heroic. Build the system you need, then choose the structure that fits the risk you are actually carrying.

~

End of chapter checklist

☑️ I understand why Making Tax Digital clashes with how real work actually happens

☑️ I know why turnover, not profit, decides whether I am in scope

☑️ I can see the weak points in my current system under quarterly reporting

☑️ I know the one simple change that would reduce friction for me

☑️ I understand that MTD exposes weak systems, it does not create them

☑️ I have paused to consider whether my current business structure still fits my level of risk

☑️ I know that structure is a long term decision, not a reaction to MTD

10

CASH BUFFERS, TAX SAVINGS, AND AVOIDING SHOCKS

Most tax stress has nothing to do with tax rates. It comes from surprises. This chapter is about removing them. I know this isn't technically 100% about Making Tax Digital, but it plays a huge part in making MTD feel calmer rather than painful.

A prospective client once said to me:

"I've come to your accountancy firm because apparently you can save me the most in tax."

"Ah yes," I replied. "You've heard about the special system."

> ***"There's a special system?" they asked, slightly confused.***

"Yes," I said. "It's called good bookkeeping."

"Is that the best you can do?"

The truth is, running my accountancy practice, I'm always amazed by how many clients simply miss things. Mileage is a big one, but it's not just mileage. I'll look at a profit and loss report and ask why the insurance isn't there.

"Oh, that goes out of the Mrs' account."

What on earth is a business expense doing going out of someone else's personal account? Yet I see this every day.

As small business owners, we don't have offshore structures or complex tax avoidance schemes. We're not Gary Barlow or Jimmy Carr and even those schemes didn't end well for those big name celebs.

Sometimes I genuinely wonder whether HMRC has made a huge mistake bringing in Making Tax Digital, because so many self-employed people don't currently keep good records. But then I realised something else. Software might actually force people to build proper systems and in doing so, finally claim what they're entitled to.

In a strange way, HMRC may have accidentally designed the most effective small-business "tax saving scheme" of all: good bookkeeping.

Let's look at mileage for a moment.

"I've not bothered adding my mileage up this year, I've done hardly any."

I sent a client away to add it up properly. They came back with around 1,000 miles for the year.

"See," they said. "Hardly any."

That client was a 40% taxpayer. Those miles represented around £189 in tax and NI savings. I asked how long it took.

"About an hour."

£189 an hour is a decent return by most standards.

~

By this stage in the book, I've already covered some critical foundations:

- Using a separate business bank account for business affairs. You get a debit card with this account, so use it. If you're spending on business items, use the business card.
- Good account conduct. Your daily McDonald's breakfast and pints down the pub do not go through the business account. Business card means business spend only. Don't break this rule.
- Choosing a bank with a good bank feed, so those clean, segregated transactions flow automatically into your bookkeeping software.
- Using tools like Xero and Dext to make reconciliation easier and to automate receipt capture.
- Setting up bank rules and automations to recognise and reconcile transactions for you.
- Raising sales invoices from Xero and making sure customers have your business bank details.

If you follow the approach above, you'll automatically capture around 95% of your business expenses.

If you've previously been running everything through a messy personal account, or clients occasionally pay the wrong account, raising invoices through your accounting software makes these issues far easier to spot and fix.

However, there are still some areas you need to watch out for. Things that don't naturally fit into the system.

Mileage — yes, I'm back on mileage again. This happens in your personal car, not through the business account, so you need a separate way to record it. It doesn't sit neatly in most accounting software. I'm not brilliant at tracking mileage, but I am good at keeping my calendar up to date. That means I can produce a mileage log at the end of the month or year. Clients who do a lot of miles often use apps like MileIQ, which track mileage automatically.

Annual payments — once you move to a business bank account, monthly payments are easy to spot when moving everything, but annual payments are often forgotten. Keep an eye out for them.

Home office use — take a reasonable amount. This is another off-system item that needs thought. Reasonable is the key word. Being too aggressive here can affect your capital gains tax position when you sell your home. Done properly, the number is usually underwhelming.

Broadband — if you work entirely from home, it's reasonable to claim a portion of the cost. Not all of it.

Travel tickets — if, like me, you only travel occasionally for work, you probably pay personally using parking or train apps. These are linked to personal accounts, so you need to remember to put business expenses through Dext.

Mobile phones — many people started their business with a phone already paid from a personal account. You can't run a business without a phone, so this needs to be dealt with properly.

. . .

Entertaining — client entertaining is disallowable. But it's sometimes hard to distinguish between entertaining and subsistence while travelling for work. Be clear with your adviser which is which.

I could go on, but the point is this: you might have built an excellent system that captures 95% of your expenses automatically, but there will always be a handful that require discipline and awareness. Not all advisers are good at flagging these. Some firms will simply say, "You're paying us to prepare the documents." Be clear about what service you're actually getting.

Top tip

An expense is usually allowable if it's incurred wholly and exclusively for business purposes. A client once asked if he could deduct the cost of his haircut. For a finance broker, the answer is no, a standard haircut isn't required for the job. But if he were a professional dancer, haircuts specifically required for performances would be allowable. ***Context matters.***

~

Why Tax Shocks Happen

If you've set up your software properly and followed the guidance in this book, you'll be capturing your income and expenses accurately. That alone doesn't guarantee you won't get a tax shock but it gives you visibility.

The main risk points are:

Income not tracked

I've seen countless new clients arrive saying, "Help, I've gone over the VAT threshold." This is one of the worst mistakes you can make. Running a monthly profit and loss report helps you see this coming. At the time of writing, VAT registration is required once your rolling 12-month turnover exceeds £90,000. If you're turning over £7,500 a month or more, seek advice early. VAT is complex and needs professional input.

Profit not reviewed

Your profit and loss tells you how much money you've made. Raymond comes to mind. When he started his painting business, he quickly realised he wasn't saving for tax. If you make money, you owe tax. Save every month. Keep it in a separate savings account and, ideally, link that account into your bookkeeping software via a bank feed.

Cash spent before tax is set aside

I say this a lot. It's easy to make money; it's much harder to live off the money you've made. Currently, you don't pay tax until ten months after the tax year ends. By then, you should have nearly two years' worth of tax saved. When that money sits in your main account, it's tempting to touch it. One client told me they dipped into tax savings because the boiler and the car both failed at once. If you're behind, understand the shortfall but keeping tax money separate creates a powerful psychological barrier.

Lack of knowledge

At the time of writing, the personal allowance is £12,570, the 40% tax band starts at £50,270, and child benefit begins to be clawed back at £60,000. A little knowledge goes a long way. Tax shocks often come from phrases like, "I didn't realise it worked like that."

Under annual reporting, shocks arrived once a year. If tax always feels like a shock to you, MTD is actually a benefit. Quarterly updates give you visibility. Each one is a chance to stop and ask:

- What is my profit so far?
- Have I saved enough tax?
- Is there a risk I'll move into a higher tax band?

The Simplest Rule That Works

Set aside 30% of your income for tax.

This isn't precision planning. It's a buffer.

For some people it will be too much. If you're in CIS, you might only need to save 10%.

The key is building the habit.

I helped a client negotiate a payment plan with HMRC after they buried their head in the sand. A £36,000 bill had grown to over £40,000 once penalties and interest were added. The damage wasn't the tax, it was the avoidance of the issue.

The Calm Conclusion

MTD can actually put people back in control. You can't avoid the numbers anymore. People stop fearing software and start making better decisions.

Making Tax Digital is often blamed for stress. In reality, it exposes habits that were already fragile.

The people who adapt best aren't the most technical. They're the ones who:

- Separate cash
- Review regularly
- Accept reality early

Once you do that, tax becomes boring. And boring is the goal.

End-of-Chapter Checklist

✅ I understand why tax shocks happen
✅ I know why a buffer matters more than accuracy
✅ I have a plan to separate tax money
✅ I understand how MTD improves visibility

PART 5. LANDLORDS WITHOUT THE FLUFF

11

MTD LANDLORD FUNDAMENTALS

Just prior to publication, HMRC issued guidance for jointly owned property. Under this guidance, rental income is reported quarterly, but expenses can be submitted at the year-end finalisation stage. Each owner still has their own Making Tax Digital obligations and submits their own figures. I would expect this guidance to change in future as the regime beds in. If your system is well thought out and set up properly, I would still submit both income and expenses each quarter.

In Chapter 7, I talked about system design and the need to think about how money flows through a business as:

Inputs → System → Delivery → Outcomes → Money

I can almost hear a few landlords shaking their heads at this point. But the same logic applies to you. A property portfolio is still a system. You have inputs, processes, delivery, outcomes, and money flowing through the whole thing.

If, like me, you use the same suppliers repeatedly in your

property business, you are already thinking in systems. I use the same people because I know how they work. They fit my processes. The work gets done properly. The tenants are happier. Happier tenants pay on time and stay longer.

Good landlord plus happy tenants leads to better results.

This is why I have covered sole traders and landlords in the same book. The underlying mechanism is the same, even if the work looks different on the surface.

Many landlords do not think of themselves as business owners. They see themselves as people renting out a spare property, long-term investors, or sometimes accidental landlords. But the way HMRC views your activity matters far more than how you label yourself.

How HMRC Defines a "Property Business"

HMRC does not share the view that landlords are just "investors" or people renting out a spare property. In this case, I agree with them. If you receive rental income, HMRC considers you to be running a property business. That language matters under Making Tax Digital.

For MTD purposes, HMRC groups your properties as follows:

- All UK rental properties are treated as one UK property business.
- All overseas rental properties are treated as one overseas property business.

This can surprise landlords. Overseas rental income is included when HMRC looks at your total qualifying income, which can matter if, for example, you are also a sole trader and close to the MTD threshold.

Note for non-residents: If you are not a UK tax resident, Making Tax Digital looks only at the income you report on your UK tax return. In practice, that means UK property income and any UK self-employment or UK land trading income you declare. Foreign rental income and overseas self-employment income that are not reported on your UK return do not count towards the MTD thresholds. So, if you live in France, rent out a property in the UK, and run a business in France, only the UK rental income is relevant for Making Tax Digital.

Fundamentally, it does not matter whether you own one flat, three houses, or a mixed portfolio. From HMRC's perspective, the reporting framework is the same.

Owning Property vs Running a Property Business

As a small business owner, I found comfort in owning property. A physical asset you can drive to and touch has real appeal. You can exert control over it and make decisions. But if, like me, you sometimes feel like the latest cash cow for the government, this chapter is for you.

Moving to cloud-based accounting software was game changing for me as a portfolio landlord. With a few clicks, I can run a report on a single property. Is it profitable? What is the rental yield? Which costs are creeping up. That visibility changes how you manage property.

Landlords often underestimate how different their world looks to HMRC.

Not in terms of tax rates.

But in terms of structure.

Making Tax Digital does not care whether you feel like a

"proper landlord" or just someone with a spare property. It cares whether you are running a property business.

This chapter is about that shift in perspective. The difference between owning one property and running a property business is not emotional. It is structural. And Making Tax Digital treats both through the same lens.

How HMRC Sees Rental Activity in Practice

This often surprises landlords. People with a single property tend to behave very differently from portfolio landlords. Single-property landlords often rely on minimal record keeping, an annual tidy-up, and bank statements as evidence. Under annual reporting, this was survivable. Memory filled the gaps and year-end adjustments masked small errors. Under quarterly reporting, that buffer disappears. Timing starts to matter. Gaps show up quickly. What used to be a slightly messy system becomes visibly fragile.

Portfolio landlords usually have better processes, simply because they have to. There are more transactions, more repairs, and often letting agents involved. But with that scale comes complexity. A common trap I see is portfolio landlords assuming, "We already do this properly." Quarterly reporting has a habit of exposing weak links in systems that felt fine when reviewed once a year. The rules have not changed, but the frequency has, and frequency changes behaviour.

Why Making Tax Digital Treats Everyone the Same

HMRC designs systems for consistency, not fairness. It does not want multiple rule sets, special cases, or subjective thresholds. Whether you own one property or ten, the reporting framework is the same. This keeps compliance predictable from HMRC's point of view, even if it feels blunt from yours. The difference between a single property and a portfolio under Making Tax Digital is not compliance. It is load. More properties mean more transactions, more receipts, and more review time. The rules do not change. The volume does. That is why systems matter more as portfolios grow.

Under Making Tax Digital, properties are also grouped. UK rental properties are treated as one UK property business. Overseas rental properties are treated as a separate overseas property business. You do not submit a quarterly update for each property. You submit one update per property business. When this is set up properly in your software, reporting becomes simpler than many landlords expect.

Where Landlords Commonly Go Wrong

The same problems appear again and again. Personal and business money is mixed in the same bank account, which destroys clarity and makes quarterly reporting painful. Timing is ignored, with repairs and rent falling into different quarters and no one quite sure why the numbers look odd. Letting agents are treated as "the system", rather than as one input into the system. Agents help, but they do not run your records. Making Tax Digital assumes you control the flow of information and review it regularly.

The Quiet Shift Making Tax Digital Creates

Making Tax Digital changes the relationship many landlords have with their properties. Property stops being something that "ticks along in the background" and becomes something you actively monitor. That can feel intrusive at first. Over time, it becomes reassuring. You stop guessing how your properties are performing. You start seeing it.

The reality check is simple. Whether you like it or not, HMRC treats property as a business. Making Tax Digital treats it as such. Systems are no longer optional. The size of your portfolio does not change that. Preparation does.

End-of-Chapter Checklist

☑ I understand that HMRC treats rental income as a property business

☑ I know how HMRC groups UK and overseas properties

☑ I understand why one property and portfolios are treated the same

☑ I can see where landlords commonly go wrong under quarterly reporting

12

REPORTING REALITIES UNDER MAKING TAX DIGITAL (INCLUDING JOINTLY HELD PROPERTIES)

This chapter looks at how reporting actually works under Making Tax Digital, not just in theory, but in the real world.

Before getting into joint ownership specifically, it covers some common reporting challenges that catch people out, including letting agents, timing differences, and how transactions appear in accounting software. These issues affect many landlords, whether they own property alone or with others.

The final sections focus specifically on jointly held properties and how reporting works when ownership is shared. If you only own property in your own name, you can skip those sections without losing valuable information.

Letting Agents Do Not Fix MTD

Letting agents add another layer of confusion. Agents often collect the rent, deduct costs, and provide neat annual statements that appear to summarise everything neatly in one place. This can give the impression that the compliance burden has been handled.

It hasn't. Letting agents do not submit MTD updates, decide tax splits, or maintain your digital records in the way Making Tax Digital requires. Their statements are inputs, useful ones, but they are not the system itself. Responsibility always sits with the individual owner.

Did you know that letting agents are regularly required to submit information to HMRC about who they have paid during the tax year? These powers come from the Finance Act and mean HMRC can cross-check what agents report against what landlords declare.

Letting agents also make reconciliation slightly more awkward in practice. A rent of £850 with a 12% management fee deducted often appears on the bank feed as £748. The correct treatment is still to record rental income of £850 with an expense of £102 for the agent's fee. If you only record the net £748 as income, your figures will not tie up properly and can create mismatches later.

In months where there are no repair deductions, you can use simple automation, such as bank rules, to handle this cleanly in your accounting software. The key point is to gross rents up to the full £850, rather than reporting the net £748. That discipline prevents confusion and keeps your records aligned with what HMRC expects to see.

Timing Issues That Catch People Out

Joint ownership also exposes timing problems much more quickly than annual reporting ever did.

A while ago, I had a £1,000 repair at a rental property. The monthly rent was £850 and the management fee was

£102. The letting agent issued a statement asking me to pay £252 to them. On a spreadsheet, this sort of adjustment is relatively straightforward. You can see the column of numbers and understand that, for that month, the property effectively made a loss of £252.

Within accounting software such as Xero, it can require a bit more thought. These systems are built around dates, periods, and bank transactions, not visual summaries. What feels obvious on a spreadsheet needs to be translated into something the software understands.

Now take the example a step further. Imagine the agent knew the £1,000 repair was coming and decided to hold back the previous month's rent to cover it. When the following month's rent arrives, they issue a single statement. The result is a payment of £496 into the bank, but that payment actually relates to two different months.

If you are working mainly from bank reconciliations, this kind of timing difference can be confusing. You suddenly need to record income and expenses across two months from a single bank line dated in one month. For someone without a financial background, this can feel unintuitive.

There are different ways to deal with this. An accountant might use journals or balance sheet control accounts to spread amounts correctly across periods. For a landlord doing their own bookkeeping, raising sales invoices to force rent into the correct months is often a more practical solution.

The approach matters less than the outcome: the figures need to reflect reality. A simple sense-check is to look at the profit and loss report month by month. If it broadly matches what you expect, the adjustments are doing their job.

Under annual reporting, these mismatches were often

smoothed out at year end. Under quarterly reporting, they become visible immediately. That may mean making occasional adjustments in the software. Modern accounting platforms have made reconciliation far easier than it once was, but edge cases like this still exist.

It's worth keeping this in perspective. The example above is rare. In my case, it has happened only twice in seven years. However, landlords with older properties or higher levels of maintenance may see timing issues like this more often. The key point is not to panic, but to recognise why quarterly reporting exposes these situations and to deal with them calmly when they arise.

Capital Improvements: Why Timing and Treatment Matter

One area where Making Tax Digital often exposes uncertainty is capital improvements.

The distinction itself is not new. Repairs are generally deductible against rental income. Capital improvements are not. They are added to the cost of the property and only come into play when the property is sold. Making Tax Digital does not change this distinction, but quarterly reporting makes it harder to gloss over.

In practice, confusion usually arises when larger works are carried out. Replacing a broken boiler with a like-for-like model is typically a repair. Installing central heating where none existed before is a capital improvement.

The tax rules have not changed, but under Making Tax Digital the way these costs are recorded matters more. These amounts now sit visibly in your software rather than being quietly corrected at year end. In the past, it was common for capital elements to be identified later from a list of repairs and dealt with through working papers. Under MTD, that tidy-up approach becomes harder to rely on.

Recording capital improvements correctly at the point they occur avoids confusion later and keeps quarterly figures meaningful.

How I Record Capital Improvements in Xero

From a bookkeeping perspective, capital improvements should not go through the profit and loss account.

In Xero, I typically record these costs to a balance sheet account, often labelled something like "**Capital Improvements**" within the fixed assets section of the chart of accounts. The invoice is entered and paid as normal, or if the cost appears only as a bank transaction it is reconciled in the usual way. The key difference is that, instead of coding it to repairs or maintenance, it is coded to this asset account.

Although I refer to Xero here, the principle applies to all accounting software. The fundamentals of management accounting are the same, regardless of the platform being used.

This achieves two things:

- Your quarterly profit figures are not distorted by costs that are not allowable deductions.
- You build up a clear, auditable record of capital expenditure that will be needed later for capital gains calculations.

There is no requirement to depreciate these costs for tax purposes, and in most cases it is not a good idea to do so.

The balance simply sits on the balance sheet until the property is sold or the figures are needed by your accountant.

The key principle is consistency. Once you decide how capital improvements are recorded, apply that approach every time.

A small complication arises when a property is sold, as these costs need to be removed from the asset account at that point. In practice, this is usually an adjustment best handled by an accountant.

For landlords with more than one property, it can feel frustrating that all capital improvements sit in a single place within the software. At that point, it becomes helpful to introduce a slightly more advanced reporting principle.

Using Tracking Categories to Keep Properties Separate

As portfolios grow, a common source of confusion is not knowing which property has made or lost money, especially when everything runs through one bank account. Being able to run reports showing capital improvement spend by property can bring immediate clarity.

Xero's tracking categories (sometimes called cost centres in other software) are a simple way of solving this without running separate sets of books. Some landlords try to keep control by using different bank accounts for each property, but with software like Xero combined with tracking categories, that level of complexity is usually unnecessary.

A common setup is to create a tracking category called "**Property**", with one option per property. Rental income and expenses are then coded as normal, but with the relevant property selected each time.

Used properly, this allows you to:

- See profit and loss by property
- Spot problem properties early
- Understand whether timing issues are genuine or just reporting noise

Tracking categories are optional. They are not required for Making Tax Digital. But for landlords with more than one property, they often turn vague concerns into clear information.

The important thing is restraint. One tracking category is usually enough. Overcomplicating the setup creates more work without adding clarity.

Each tracking category adds an extra step to every transaction, so it's best used only where it genuinely adds value, typically when you have more than one property.

Top tip: In my own setup, I use the tracking category suggested above (for example, **"Properties"**) with each property listed as an option. I also include an additional option called **"Office Costs"**.

Some costs, such as accounting fees, cannot sensibly be split across individual properties. These are assigned to the "Office Costs" option instead. This allows me to run a report each quarter showing any items that have not been assigned to a specific property.

In Xero, these appear as **"Unassigned"**. In practice, this highlights transactions I have missed or not yet categorised. If the list is longer than expected, I use Xero's Find & Recode tool to quickly assign those items to the correct place.

How This Fits with Making Tax Digital

Neither capital improvements nor tracking categories

are new concepts. What Making Tax Digital does is remove the ability to ignore them.

Quarterly reporting means:

- Capital costs need to be clearly separated from repairs
- Property performance becomes visible sooner
- Weak categorisation shows up repeatedly, not once a year

Handled well, this reduces surprises. Handled poorly, it creates ongoing friction.

Why Making Tax Digital Exposes Weak Records

Making Tax Digital does not change what landlords can claim or how tax works. What it changes is when problems surface.

The examples so far illustrate two things. First, how regular reporting can provide more useful insight into how a property business is actually performing. Second, where complications tend to arise when records, timing, or responsibilities are unclear.

As with everything in this chapter, the goal is not perfection. It is a system that reflects reality and can be maintained calmly over time.

Under annual reporting, weak records could survive for years. Mistakes were absorbed by year-end adjustments. Chapter 15 builds on this by setting out practical ways to review your figures and sense-check that the information being reported is sound.

This particularly affects landlords who relied on end-of-year tidy-ups, letting agent statements, or bank statements alone. Income and costs become visible when they arise, not when they are later explained. The rules have not changed, but they are applied more frequently and with less room for assumption.

Joint Ownership Feels Simple, Until It Isn't

Joint ownership feels obvious. Two people own a property together. The rent comes in. The bills go out. The profit belongs to both of them. It feels natural to assume that the reporting works the same way.

In practice, many couples or co-owners operate on exactly that assumption. One person deals with the paperwork. One spreadsheet exists. One tax return becomes the "main" one, and the other person simply mirrors it. Under annual reporting, this approach often went unchallenged. Under Making Tax Digital, it doesn't.

The reason is simple. HMRC does not see a jointly owned property as a single taxable unit. It never has. It sees two separate taxpayers who happen to own an interest in the same asset. Making Tax Digital doesn't change the law, but it removes the places where informal arrangements used to hide.

Each owner must submit their own quarterly updates and final declaration through their own HMRC account. You can use the same accountant and even the same software, but you cannot make one submission and treat it as covering both people.

This gap between how joint ownership feels and how it is taxed is where most problems start. Rent might be paid into one person's account. Costs might be paid by the other.

Repairs might fall into a different quarter from the rent they relate to. Under annual reporting, these mismatches were often smoothed out later. Under quarterly reporting, they surface immediately.

The Default Split and When It Changes

Unless something different has been formally put in place, HMRC assumes that income and expenses from jointly owned property are split equally. This default 50:50 split applies whether the owners are married, in a civil partnership, or completely unrelated.

That default only changes if the underlying beneficial ownership is genuinely different and has been properly declared. In other words, the split must reflect reality, not convenience. There must be evidence to support it, and HMRC must be formally notified where required.

As a practical aside, we often suggest a deed of trust to create an unequal split where one spouse is a lower earner. In that case, Form 17 must be filed with HMRC within 60 days of the deed being executed, so HMRC is aware of the different ownership split.

Making Tax Digital does not introduce new rules here. It simply makes existing ones more visible, more frequent, and harder to ignore.

A common assumption is that one person "does the tax" and the other just follows along. Under Making Tax Digital, that habit breaks as each owner submits their own figures under their own HMRC account. You can share the work. You cannot share the responsibility.

What Good Looks Like in Practice

A clean joint ownership setup doesn't need to be complicated, but it does need agreement. In practice, that usually means a clear flow of money, agreed responsibility for expenses, regular review points, and software that works for both owners.

Problems arise when one person is organised and engaged while the other assumes it all "just works". Making Tax Digital forces alignment. That can feel uncomfortable at first, but it is far easier to address this early than to fight it every quarter.

The Practical Takeaway

Making Tax Digital rewards clarity and engagement. It does not change how landlords are taxed, but it does require each individual to take responsibility for their own reporting.

Where property is jointly owned, that responsibility cannot be assumed or delegated informally. Each owner has their own obligations, must be set up correctly, and must engage with the process in their own right. Letting agents, spreadsheets, or shared records can support that process, but they do not replace it.

Handled well, this brings transparency, regular communication, and clearer ownership of responsibilities. The adjustment can feel uncomfortable at first, but over time joint ownership becomes manageable rather than stressful. The goal is not perfection, but fewer surprises and calmer reporting.

End-of-Chapter Checklist

☑ I understand that Making Tax Digital requires individual responsibility for reporting

☑ I know that letting agents and statements are inputs, not a reporting system

☑ I understand how timing differences can affect quarterly figures

☑ I know why clean, current records matter more under MTD

☑ I understand that each joint owner reports separately and must be set up correctly

☑ I know what a clean, workable system looks like for jointly held property

13

LIMITED COMPANIES, SECTION 24 AND MTD

Many landlords experience Making Tax Digital as the latest attack on them. Writing a book on MTD is one thing but I wanted to end this part of the book about you landlords with some deeper strategy.

My wife owns a single rental property, which makes her a useful real world example. In the 2024 to 2025 tax year, she came close to paying as much tax as the net profit the property actually made. If you are an experienced landlord, you will know exactly what that feels like.

That pressure exists because:

- Mortgage interest relief has already been restricted.
- Taxable profits and real world cash profits no longer match.
- Thresholds are crossed more easily, which claws back benefits and allowances. Tax bills feel disconnected from reality.

I have seen a number of clients who have received rental

income for years while remaining basic rate taxpayers. As wage inflation has accelerated and rental prices have jumped over the last few years, they have suddenly been hit by the restriction of finance costs.

In simple terms, rents that were once £650 a month are now £1,000 a month. In cases like my wife's, this has pushed people into the 40% tax band. At the same time, the Bank of England base rates jumped. The result was a perfect storm.

I had warned clients about the impact of mortgage interest restrictions, but while they were basic rate taxpayers, the end result still felt manageable. Once pay rises, higher rents, and higher mortgage costs arrived at the same time, the tax bill quickly became out of proportion to what they felt they had actually earned.

So you are probably in one of two camps as a landlord. Either you do not really understand how the system works, or you already understand it and hate it.

I could not write this chapter without touching on structural choices for landlords. At the same time, if you are a new or inexperienced landlord, some of the ideas in this chapter may feel challenging. That is fine.

Going back to my wife she is outside the scope of Making Tax Digital because the rental income is modest. If the same property were in the South of England, the rent would likely be high enough to push her into the MTD thresholds, at least by April 2027.

Then Making Tax Digital arrives and asks landlords to engage with this more often.

The tax problem remains the same. The administrative burden increases.

As a landlord, it is natural to feel targeted. It is also important to be precise about what is actually happening.

Making Tax Digital does not change how landlords are

taxed. Section 24 still applies. Tax rates still apply. Allowances still apply.

What Making Tax Digital changes is visibility. Quarterly updates force you to look at your numbers more often. They surface the gap between cash profit and taxable profit earlier in the year. They bring forward the emotional impact of rules that were previously felt once a year.

The real source of frustration for landlords

The frustration most landlords feel does not come from software.

It comes from distortion.

Under Section 24:

- Mortgage interest is no longer fully deductible.
- Taxable income is inflated.
- Tax thresholds are breached more easily.
- Effective tax rates can jump sharply.

A 2% tax increase is round the corner, tax free allowances for CGT have been slashed and landlords feel trapped. I'm already seeing landlords making the wrong decisions or putting in place structures that don't work.

Making Tax Digital does not create distortion. It removes the ability to ignore it until January. Seeing the same problem four times a year can feel like harassment. It is not. It is feedback and with regular feedback we can make solid business decisions.

Why incorporation is often discussed

My portfolio is partially held in a limited company and some in my personal name. So I'm not writing this section as an accountant who has never actually done what I'm writing about. Other accountants might even pick up this book and be reassured by my approach. As dealing with property assets creates huge financial decisions and quite often big tax liabilities at the same time.

So as a landlord you're probably asking:

> ***"I've heard a limited company is the way forward. Is it?"***

I get it! It is easy to see why this idea is attractive. Owning property through a limited company allows:

- Full deduction of mortgage interest.
- Profits to be taxed at lower corporation tax rates starting at 19%.
- More control over when income is taken personally.
- The option to retain profits for reinvestment.

This is why company ownership has grown so quickly among landlords. It is a rational response to Section 24, not a trend.

On paper, this can look compelling. But moving existing property into a company without using a complex partnership structure will trigger capital gains tax (CGT) and Stamp Duty Land Tax (SDLT).

> ***So does that mean we should avoid limited companies?***

With MTD your software is capable of running real time profit and loss reports on each property. I talked about how to setup tracking categories in the last chapter. Yes, it's extra work when you are doing your bookkeeping but for a portfolio landlord it makes a huge difference to determine if a company might work.

Let me give you another example. I was with my client Lewis and he'd been using Xero for his property portfolio and using tracking categories. We created P&L reports for each property in terms of:

- Can rental income be increased?
- Are the mortgage deals the best we can achieve?
- Which properties are costing money?
- What's the overall trend over multiple years?

Then one property we reviewed came up and Lewis said "Oh I used to live in that property?" That grabbed my attention.

The period of residency was long and would more than likely cover 80% of the capital gains on the property. Maybe this could be an option to move into his property company?

The property was worth around £190,000 and had originally been purchased for £145,000. Ignoring any periods of residence, the gain would therefore have been subject to capital gains tax at up to 24%.

Moving a property into a company triggers both capital gains tax and stamp duty land tax, which can make incorporation an expensive decision. In this case, the monthly rent was £1,300 and the SDLT bill came to £10,800.

Despite the upfront cost, the client decided it was worthwhile in the long term. The rental margin, the impact of personal tax at higher rates, and his position around the

£100,000 income threshold where the personal allowance is lost all meant that paying the SDLT upfront produced a better long-term outcome.

Without proper bookkeeping software, we would never have been able to review the portfolio in this level of detail. Having clear, consistent records meant we could see the true rental margins, and because the restriction on finance costs under section 24 was such a significant factor, we were able to analyse that element carefully.

While the client kept their records organised, it also allowed their professional adviser to step in and model the wider tax consequences including stamp duty land tax, capital gains tax, personal allowance restrictions, and the impact of section 24 before any decision was made. To be clear it would still take many years for this move to repay the upfront costs.

Another benefit was that the client had been using Xero consistently for many years. As discussed in the previous chapter, capital improvements recorded properly in the software can make a material difference later.

While reviewing the capital improvements account, I noted a small kitchen extension carried out several years earlier. The client's reaction was telling: *"Oh, I'd forgotten about that."*

That moment is very familiar. Over the last fifteen years, I've seen many landlords hand over unnecessary capital gains tax simply because improvements were forgotten or poorly documented. When portfolios grow, it becomes impossible to remember every decision made with an accountant a decade earlier, or how specific costs were treated at the time.

In this case, those historic records changed the outcome entirely. When we revisited the figures as part of the incorporation decision, the position moved from capital gains tax being due to no capital gains tax being payable at all.

That is the real value of good records. They don't just support compliance. They protect you from paying tax you don't actually owe.

When I started working with one client he came to me because of the relatively new reporting rules on CGT about needing to report and pay within 60 days.

"Do you have the completion statement when you bought the property?" I asked.

> ***"No, of course I don't, I bought it in 1986!" the client said bemused.***

I wanted to look at them to see what the legal costs might be. But these are usually small values compared to the capital improvement costs. When I enquired of the client about these costs he was proud to tell me about an attic conversion he'd done in the late 90s. But he had no records.

"I thought you only needed to keep records for 6 years." the client said.

That isn't actually true when it comes to capital improvements, because those records need to be kept long term. This is one area where good software can make a dramatic difference.

Going back to my client Lewis, we were able to click a few buttons and see the tracked balance sheet account for capital improvements. That figure was exactly the amount we could apply against the capital gain, and it immediately brought the forgotten kitchen extension back into view.

While this is a huge improvement to what I've seen in the past I do see an issue with software solutions. If you cancel a receipt scanning software solution like Dext they will keep your records for 6 years. Brilliant that's HMRC compliant but actually you could end up losing your capital improvement costs evidence. While Xero is my brand of choice today that might not be the case 5-10 years from now. Services like Move My Books will allow you to move a few years of data and then they ask for a fee to move the rest. While the balance of your capital improvements nominal will transfer the transaction details might not. So it's really important to think about capital improvements as I do think there is a risk of data loss.

Before even considering company ownership, a detailed analysis is needed. This includes the tax implications of selling and repurchasing property, as well as a clear understanding of how historic information has been recorded.

But Why Companies?

Company ownership is often presented as a solution to landlord tax problems, particularly in the context of Section 24. It can be effective in the right circumstances, but it is not a decision to be made casually.

Incorporation is not just a tax calculation. It involves transaction taxes, long-term record keeping, financing implications, and practical administration. Making Tax Digital should not be the driver of that decision. At most, it acts as a spotlight, exposing whether existing structures are still fit for purpose.

This is not something to decide over a quick cup of tea. Structure is a long-term choice, and while tax is an important factor, it should never be the only one.

It affects:

- Borrowing costs - these can be more expensive
- Mortgage availability - fewer lenders
- Personal guarantees - you still owe the money ultimately
- Admin burden - it costs more to run a property company
- Succession planning - it's not classed as a trading business
- How easily profits can be accessed.

Just remember. A limited company is not a tax wrapper. It is a long term ownership structure. I'm not writing a book on how you can restructure but I am an accountant who owns property personally and via a company.

For many portfolios, the upfront tax cost is so large that the payback period is simply too long to justify the move with CGT and SDLT being triggered on the transfer.

This leaves many landlords in a frustrating position. They can see a structure that may be more efficient going forward. They cannot move to it without triggering large one off tax bills.

Making Tax Digital does not change this reality. It simply makes the trade offs harder to ignore.

What Making Tax Digital changes in real life for landlords

Making Tax Digital changes rhythm, not rules.

You will see:

- Rental income and costs more often.
- Taxable profit figures more often.

- Threshold impacts earlier in the year.
- The cash versus tax gap sooner.

This can be uncomfortable. It can also be useful.

- Earlier visibility allows:
- Earlier cash planning.
- Earlier tax saving.
- Fewer January surprises.
- Calmer decisions on exit or restructure

For landlords who feel stuck structurally, the value is not in changing structure. It is in improving awareness and planning within the structure you already have.

What this chapter is and is not saying

This chapter is not telling you to incorporate. It is not telling you to restructure your portfolio. It is not suggesting MTD changes the tax rules.

What I would be doing is using software like Xero even if you are below the first deadline date. Why? Because it's going to provide your information on margin, rental income, profit and highlight issues around section 24.

But before reaching for a limited company as the be all and end all. Consider these ideas. As if I was an unincorporated landlord I'd maybe discuss these things with my accountant:

- For married couples - look at existing ownership structures as you can benefit from no gain no loss transfers away from solely held to joint names.

- Deeds of trust - these are especially handy if you are a married couple as you can divert income away from a higher earner in the relationship.
- Maximising commercial borrowing so you can pay down restricted residential finance costs affected by Section 24.
- Partnerships - it's still possible to use a partnership to incorporate your property business but you need specialist advice. Please be careful as these schemes attract big fees and I'm often dubious of some advisors. It's also not something I advise on.
- Creating your own management company - larger landlords have formed in effect their own letting agency. It's not open to the public but some have staff who manage the properties. This not only creates an expense for the personally held properties but your new property management company holds these profits being taxed at a lower level.

Calm conclusion for landlords

MTD reflects the system you are already in. For some landlords, the right response is structural change. For many, the right response is better planning, better cash flow management, and better routines.

The mistake is to treat MTD as the problem. The problem is the mismatch between cash reality and tax rules. MTD just makes that mismatch harder to ignore.

Future wages and rental income increases can push landlords who maybe only paid tax at 20% into 40%.

If you want to go deeper on whether incorporation

might be useful, scan the QR code below to download my fact sheet:

~

End of chapter checklist

✅ I understand why Making Tax Digital feels like extra pressure for landlords

✅ I understand that MTD changes visibility, not the tax rules

✅ I can see the gap between cash profit and taxable profit under Section 24

✅ I understand why this gap will feel louder under quarterly reporting

✅ I know why limited companies are often discussed by landlords

✅ I understand why moving existing properties into a company can be expensive

✅ I understand that incorporation is a long term structural decision, not an MTD response

✅ I can see the value of better records and per property reporting under MTD

✅ I know that frustration with MTD is usually about tax structure, not software

PART 6. GETTING AHEAD WITHOUT LOSING WEEKENDS

14

POINTS-BASED PENALTIES, THE SOFT LANDING, AND WILL HMRC FORGIVE YOU?

Over the years I have helped many clients challenge HMRC penalties. Most of them had genuine reasons. Ill health. Family crises. Systems that broke when life did. The penalties were not always wrong in law, but the people behind them were not careless. They were overwhelmed.

What strikes me is how often people ignore problems until they become frightening. Not because they are lazy, but because they are anxious. When something feels threatening, the human response is often avoidance. That avoidance is what turns a small issue into a crisis.

One client, a railway worker with a tough exterior, came into my office because HMRC were chasing him for around £3,000 in penalties. He had the letters in his car, but he was too frightened to open them. We went through them together. He had been unwell, the appeal had merit, and HMRC cancelled the penalties.

The lesson is not that HMRC is unreasonable. The lesson is that silence makes things worse. When people do nothing, the system assumes they do not care. When people engage early, even with a problem, outcomes are often far better.

Penalties worry people more than rules. Not because the rules are harsher, but because penalties are badly explained. The language is technical. The logic is buried. People imagine the worst.

Points-based penalties

Once you understand how the penalty system actually works, most of the fear disappears. The new penalty regime is not designed to punish single mistakes. The old system did that. Miss one deadline and you were fined, even if you were usually compliant. That created resentment, not better behaviour.

This model has already been used for VAT. In practice, it has been better received by many of our clients and by other accountancy firms. The previous surcharge system was, in my view, deeply unhelpful. Moving away from it is a sensible step.

The new system for income tax is designed to respond to patterns. It distinguishes between people who occasionally slip and people who repeatedly ignore deadlines. That is a meaningful shift. It does not mean penalties go away. It means they are triggered by behaviour over time, not by one bad week.

The points-based penalty system is simple once you strip away the jargon.

Every time you miss a required submission, you earn a penalty point. If you keep missing deadlines, points build up. A financial penalty only applies once you reach a set threshold of points. Until then, you are warned through points, not fined. One slip does not cost you money. Repeated failure does. That is the logic of the system. As with VAT, you should receive a letter from HMRC when a penalty point is added.

What counts as a missed submission is also straightforward. Under Making Tax Digital, each quarterly update has a deadline. If it is submitted late, that is a missed submission. The final declaration at the end of the tax year also has a deadline. If that is late, it counts too. Each type of obligation is tracked separately, but the principle does not change. Deadlines are real. Missing them has consequences.

The key reassurance for most people is this. You do not get hit with a financial penalty the first time something goes wrong. Money is only charged once you build up enough points to cross the threshold. That threshold is set to strike a balance. It is low enough to nudge people into better habits, but high enough to allow for the reality of life. HMRC is not expecting perfection. It is looking for consistency.

Points do not hang over you forever. The system is designed to allow recovery. Points reset once two things happen. First, you bring everything up to date. Second, you then submit on time for a sustained period. In other words, the system does not trap you. It gives you a way back to zero through improved behaviour. That is deliberate. The goal is better habits, not permanent punishment.

Just remember: the system is designed to respond to patterns, not one bad week.

Where people get caught out is rarely the first missed deadline. It is what happens next. People miss one update, feel embarrassed or overwhelmed, and then avoid the system. One missed deadline turns into two. Two turns into a pattern. By the time they re-engage, points have built up and penalties feel inevitable. The penalty system does not create this problem. Weak systems and avoidance do. The points-based system simply makes that pattern visible.

The 2026 to 2027 soft landing

One of the most misunderstood parts of Making Tax Digital is the so-called soft landing. Some people hear the phrase and assume Making Tax Digital is optional at first. Others assume nothing really happens in the first year. Both interpretations are wrong.

The soft landing is narrow. For the 2026 to 2027 tax year, people joining Making Tax Digital from April 2026 will not receive late submission penalties for quarterly updates. The obligation to submit still exists. The requirement to keep digital records still exists. The only thing that is delayed is one specific penalty. Nothing else is switched off.

This does not make Making Tax Digital optional. It does not give you a free year. It does not mean you can wait to build systems. HMRC still expects digital records to be kept. The final declaration still has deadlines. Late payment rules still apply. HMRC can still intervene if records are poor. The absence of one type of penalty does not equal immunity from compliance.

The soft landing exists for practical reasons, not generosity. HMRC knows that millions of people are changing systems at the same time. Software learning curves are real. Early mistakes are inevitable. Removing immediate penalties for late quarterly updates reduces panic and noise in the first year. It does not remove responsibility. The rules are live from day one. Only the consequences of one type of failure are delayed.

The most dangerous way to read the soft landing is this.

"I'll see how it goes in the first year." That mindset creates weak habits and fragile systems. It turns a practice period into procrastination. By April 2027, penalties switch on, expectations harden, and tolerance drops. People who coast through the soft landing tend to find the second year far more painful than it needs to be.

Used properly, the soft landing is a practice year. It is a chance to build habits without the pressure of points building up. It is the year to fix workflows, reduce friction, learn your software, and review routines. Mistakes made early are cheap. Mistakes repeated later are not.

From April 2027, the points-based penalty system applies in full. Late submissions begin to earn points. Repeated failures turn into financial penalties. Points only reset once behaviour improves. The soft landing does not change how that system works. It simply delays when it starts to bite.

Prepared people barely notice the soft landing. They submit on time anyway. They use the year to refine their system. For them, April 2027 is uneventful.

What HMRC will and will not forgive

HMRC is often described as unforgiving. That is only partly true. HMRC does forgive mistakes. What it does not forgive is patterns of non-compliance. Under Making Tax Digital, that distinction matters more than ever because behaviour is visible more often. Quarterly reporting makes patterns obvious very quickly.

HMRC understands that people are human, that systems fail, and that learning curves exist. This is especially true in the early stages of adopting Making Tax Digital. A missed deadline that is followed by prompt correction is usually treated as a mistake. A genuine software problem that is fixed quickly is usually treated as a mistake. An error that you identify yourself and correct voluntarily is usually treated as a mistake. These situations share a common feature. They are isolated. They are acknowledged. They are not repeated. HMRC looks at behaviour over time, not one bad moment.

What HMRC does not forgive is ongoing disengagement. Repeated late submissions, ignored reminders, and poor records quarter after quarter tell a different story. When explanations change but outcomes do not, it signals that the system is not being taken seriously. Making Tax Digital is designed to surface this kind of behaviour. It does not create the problem. It reveals it.

There is a harder reality to accept. Once a system is live and established, "I didn't know" carries far less weight. HMRC has spent years writing to taxpayers, publishing guidance, phasing implementation, and giving notice. By April 2026, unfamiliarity on its own becomes a weak defence. That does not mean HMRC expects perfection. It expects reasonable awareness and active engagement.

It also helps to understand that HMRC treats late filing and poor records very differently. Late filing is visible and measurable. It is handled through points and fixed penalties. Poor records undermine the integrity of the tax system itself. They suggest ongoing neglect rather than a single failure. Late filing can often be recovered from. Poor record-keeping compounds risk over time. This is why digital record-keeping is not optional under Making Tax Digital. The system relies on the quality of the data underneath it.

Reasonable excuse still exists, but it is narrower than many people expect. Serious illness, bereavement, or a major systems failure genuinely outside your control may qualify. Being busy, forgetting, disliking software, or hoping the issue would resolve itself generally will not. Making Tax Digital is built around routine. Routine failures are unlikely to be accepted as reasonable excuses.

One of the strongest signals of good faith is voluntary correction. When you identify an error yourself, fix it promptly, and change your behaviour going forward, HMRC tends to view this positively. Waiting for HMRC to raise the issue does not help. Making Tax Digital rewards engagement. It does not reward silence.

The riskiest position is not making a mistake. It is doing nothing. Ignoring letters, deadlines, and digital prompts creates a trail that is hard to defend later. Silence does not look accidental. It looks deliberate. And under a system designed to track patterns, deliberate disengagement is what attracts consequences.

Calm conclusion

If you take nothing else from this chapter, take this. The penalty system is not designed to catch you out. It is designed to change habits.

The soft landing is not a free pass. It is a chance to practise without consequences while you build a routine that works in real life. Used well, it makes the first year of Making Tax Digital calm.

HMRC is not looking for flawless records or heroic admin efforts. It is looking for steady behaviour and regular submissions using basic digital records. If something goes wrong, correct it early.

Most penalty problems I see are not caused by the rules. They are caused by silence.

End of chapter checklist

✅ I understand how the points-based penalty system works

✅ I know what counts as a missed submission

✅ I know that one mistake does not trigger a fine, patterns do

✅ I understand what the soft landing is and what it is not

✅ I know that the soft landing is a practice year, not a free year

✅ I understand what HMRC tends to forgive and what it does not

✅ I know that early engagement beats silence

✅ I know that boring routines reduce penalty risk

15

PROCESSES THAT ACTUALLY WORK UNDER MAKING TAX DIGITAL

In Chapters 7 and 8, I talked about system design and choosing software. This chapter is about what happens next. Not theory. Not features. Just the routine you follow once the system is live.

At Orange Umbrella, we build processes as simple checklists for clients, because most people do not need more information. They need a repeatable routine. Knowledge is rarely the problem. Consistency is.

Every client's setup is slightly different. Bookkeeping systems vary depending on factors such as the number of properties, bank accounts, payment providers, currencies, and connected apps in use. One landlord may have multiple rental bank accounts. Another may receive rent in euros for a property they previously lived in overseas.

Cloud software like Xero makes this possible, but it also means the process needs to flex to fit the reality. The same applies to sole traders, who might use connected apps for card payments, or tradespeople using tools like Tradify to manage jobs, with sales data feeding directly into Xero.

That is why process matters more than software features.

A good month-end or quarter-end process is not a heroic clean-up. It is a short, repeatable checklist that keeps the system behaving and prevents small issues from becoming bigger ones later.

Here is a simplified version of what we actually use with clients:

- Have all purchase invoices been captured?
- Does the bank balance in the software match the real bank?
- Are there any missing invoices behind unreconciled bank lines?
- Does the purchase ledger make sense?
- Do the sales figures broadly match reality?
- Does the profit and loss look reasonable?
- Does the balance sheet look sane?

That is not accounting brilliance. It is process. It works because it is boring. You will notice what is missing, which removes the temptation to say 'I'll fix it later'.

The minimum viable MTD process

You do not need a perfect system. You need one that works when life gets in the way. At a minimum, an MTD-ready process has four parts:

1. A separate bank account for the business or property
2. MTD capable accounting software
3. Digital receipt capture
4. A short weekly or fortnightly review habit

If you have those four things in place, you can comply with MTD without drama. Everything else is optimisation.

The boring process that wins

Here is the simple process I want you to aim for. This is what "good" looks like under MTD.

1. System before software

- You understand how money flows through your business.
- Inputs → System → Delivery → Outcomes → Money
- Your software supports how you work, not the other way round.

2. Inputs are captured cleanly

- All business money goes through one account.
- Bank feeds pull transactions in automatically.
- Receipts and bills are captured close to the time they happen.
- No retyping. No memory.

3. Processing is boring

- Transactions are coded consistently.
- Income is raised inside the software.
- Invoices match payments without detective work.
- The system reduces decisions instead of creating them.

4. Reconciliation keeps you sane

- The software bank balance matches the real bank.
- Every transaction appears once and only once.
- You reconcile little and often, not in a panic at deadlines.
- Reconciliation is a sanity check, not busywork.

5. Outputs are a consequence

- Quarterly updates feel like a review, not a rebuild.
- You trust the profit and loss and cash figures.
- Submissions are based on reconciled data, not hope.

6. Review is regular

- You pause to ask, does this look right?
- You spot gaps and patterns.
- You fix mistakes so they do not repeat.
- You review little and often, not months later.

The ten minute review before you submit

I talked about the process of review in chapter 7 and Making Tax Digital should create a new habit. Four times a year, you press submit. That moment matters more than most people realise.

Under annual reporting, errors could hide for months. By the time you noticed, the detail was gone. Quarterly reporting shortens that gap. Bad data gets locked in more often. Good habits matter more.

Before each quarterly submission, do a ten minute review.

Look at three simple views.

Profit and loss for the period

- Does this broadly match how the period felt?
- Do patterns month to month make sense?

Cash in and cash out

- Does the money movement match reality?

One line per income stream or property

For sole traders, this might be per client or job type.

For landlords, it is usually per property.

Do the numbers make sense?

If any of these look wildly wrong, do not submit yet. Something is missing, duplicated, or misclassified.

~

What to sanity check?

This is not an audit. It is a common sense check.

Ask yourself:

- Does the income look broadly right for the quarter?
- Is anything obviously missing?
- Has something been counted twice?
- Are there big costs that do not belong in this period?

- Are repairs mixed up with improvements?
- Are personal items sitting in business costs?
- Does the bank movement make sense for what you remember doing?
- Is there a large payment you cannot explain?
- Have transfers between accounts been labelled correctly?

If something feels off, it usually is.

Patterns that should make you pause

Over time, you will get used to your numbers. That is a good thing. It means patterns stand out.

Pause before submitting if:

- Profit jumps or drops with no clear reason
- Cash feels tight but profit looks high
- Repairs spike because of one big job
- Income dips because invoices were raised late
- A category that is normally active is suddenly empty

None of these are problems on their own. They are signals. Signals are useful if you notice them early.

Calm conclusion

Most people experience Making Tax Digital as administration. Numbers are submitted, fingers are crossed, and the worry is deferred until later.

A short, regular review changes that relationship. The rules stay the same, but the numbers stop being abstract.

Cash pressure becomes visible earlier. Tax builds up in a way that can be anticipated rather than feared. January stops being a shock.

This is not about bookkeeping for HMRC. Bookkeeping records the past. The habit described in this chapter is about understanding what has already happened, so it doesn't surprise you later.

Making Tax Digital rewards boring routines. Ten minutes of calm review beats hours of clean-up. The goal is not perfect numbers. It is fewer surprises.

That is how Making Tax Digital becomes manageable, even if it was never something you asked for.

End of chapter checklist

✅ I have a simple process that runs every week or fortnight

✅ My system works without relying on memory

✅ I reconcile little and often

✅ I do a ten minute review before each quarterly submission

✅ I know what "normal" looks like in my numbers

✅ I fix small issues before they become big ones

16

A 90 DAY PREPARATION PLAN

By now, you already know the rules. You understand the systems and the behaviours that Making Tax Digital quietly rewards. What you don't need is more information.

What you need is a plan.

This chapter sets out a simple 90-day preparation plan for Making Tax Digital. People arrive at Making Tax Digital from different starting points. Some are mandated in 2026, others in 2027 or 2028. Some are preparing early and methodically. Others are already partway through and have the uneasy sense that the system is running them, rather than the other way around. The timing may differ, but the preparation does not.

You may have picked up this book because something has gone wrong. Or because you are newly self-employed and want to avoid problems before they appear. Both are sensible reasons.

Step zero: Access your HMRC account

A surprising number of people do not have their HMRC online account set up. This is sometimes called a Personal Tax Account. Even fewer have ever logged into it. Under Making Tax Digital, that stops being optional.

You need an HMRC online account so your software can connect and submit updates. This is not complicated, but it catches people out because it is unfamiliar.

If you already file Self Assessment online, you probably already have a Government Gateway account. If you have always filed on paper, you may not. If your accountant has always done everything, you may not even know whether you have access. In many cases, your accountant will have been submitting via their own agent login, and they cannot simply give you access to that account.

You need:

- Your National Insurance number
- Your Government Gateway user ID and password
- Access to the email address and mobile number linked to your HMRC account

If you do not have a Government Gateway account, create one. If you have one but cannot remember the login, recover it now, not in deadline week.

Treat this like a bank login. If you cannot log in calmly today, fix that before you worry about anything else.

If you use an accountant, clarify who is responsible for this step. Many problems come from assumed responsibility. The client thinks the accountant has access. The accountant assumes the client can log in. The result is last minute panic.

. . .

Step zero - Part A: If you are new to self employment or renting

If you are newly self employed or a new landlord, you may not have any HMRC online account at all. That is normal.

Your first job is simply to create your Government Gateway login and personal tax account. This gives you access to HMRC online services and allows software to connect later.

Do this early. Account creation and identity checks can take time, especially if HMRC cannot match your details straight away. If this step is not complete, nothing else can move forward. No software can connect. No submissions can be made.

Think of this as opening the door. Until the door is open, you cannot even get into the room.

Step zero - Part B: If you already have an HMRC account, you still need to sign up for MTD

Even if you already have a Government Gateway account and file Self Assessment online, you are not automatically registered for Making Tax Digital for Income Tax.

Access and registration are different steps.

Logging in gives you access to HMRC. Signing up tells HMRC that your business or rental income is now part of Making Tax Digital.

You must **actively** register your business or property income for MTD before any software can submit quarterly updates on your behalf. Simply having an HMRC account is not enough.

If you skipped Part A, read this. *This is the step many people miss. They assume their accountant has done it. The accountant assumes the client is already registered. Everything looks fine until the first quarterly deadline arrives and nothing can be submitted.*

Once you have access to your HMRC account, the next step is to sign up your business or property income for Making Tax Digital and then connect your software. Do not leave this until deadline week. HMRC checks and confirmations can take days, sometimes longer if details do not line up.

Why 90 days is enough

Most people overestimate how long preparation takes. They imagine weeks of setup, complicated decisions, and disruption to work. In reality, most of the effort is front loaded thinking, not ongoing work.

If, like me, you are a last minute Charlie who thrives on pressure, some steps will still trip you up. Registration is the classic one. I had a client who failed the online checks and then could not pass security on the phone. He saw the funny side at first. But if it had been a few hours before a deadline, the humour runs out fast.

Ninety days is enough to build the system, test the habits, and remove friction. After that, the system runs quietly.

What happens if it goes wrong

If things go wrong with access, registration, or software connections, do not panic. I cover exactly what to do when Making Tax Digital goes wrong in the next chapter. The key point here is not to leave access and registration until deadline week.

Month 1, build the foundations

Focus: structure, not momentum

This month exists to remove uncertainty and noise. Nothing here is clever. Everything here is stabilising.

Week 1, confirm your position

Do three things and only these three things:

- Check which tax year HMRC will use to assess you
- Confirm whether April 2026 or April 2027 applies
- Accept the outcome without arguing with it

Clarity removes mental noise. Debating reality does not.

Week 2, separate your money

If you have not already, draw a line.

- Open a dedicated business or rental bank account
- Stop mixing personal and business spending
- Commit to one card, used consistently

This single step removes more problems than any software choice ever will.

. . .

Week 3, choose your core software

Choose accounting software that:

- Supports Making Tax Digital submissions
- Feels intuitive to you
- Does not overwhelm you with features

Ignore advanced tools for now. Simple beats clever at this stage.

Week 4, capture receipts properly

Decide once how receipts will enter your system. It might be photographing them immediately, emailing them in, or using a receipt app consistently. What matters is consistency, not elegance.

By the end of Month 1, your system should exist. It does not need to be perfect.

Month 2, make it routine

Focus: habits, not accuracy

This is where resistance usually appears. That is normal.

Week 5, turn on bank feeds

Connect the bank feed and expect initial mess. Old transactions may appear, and you may need some manual work to tidy it. Do not judge the system yet.

Week 6, clean as you go

Each week, review transactions, correct obvious errors,

and attach missing receipts if you already have them. Do not try to fix history. Fix forward.

Week 7, learn the only reports you need

Ignore most dashboards. Focus on three things:

- Profit and loss
- Cash balance
- Obvious trends

If you can answer "where am I" in five minutes, the system is working.

Week 8, practise the submission journey

If you can, run through a practice submission or a full rehearsal with your accountant or software provider. The goal is familiarity, not perfect numbers. Anxiety drops sharply when the process feels normal.

Month 3, reduce friction

Focus: comfort, not optimisation

Now you are no longer reacting. You are refining.

Week 9, notice what feels annoying

Pay attention to tasks you avoid, screens you dislike, or steps that feel unnecessary. Friction is feedback. Fixing small annoyances prevents future avoidance.

. . .

Week 10, automate gently

Look for repeating transactions, predictable suppliers, and regular income. Use automation sparingly. Automation supports habits. It does not replace them.

Week 11, tighten the review habit

Set a fixed time each week or fortnight. Ten to fifteen minutes is enough. Consistency matters more than depth.

Week 12, step back and assess

Ask yourself:

- Does this feel calmer than before
- Do I know where I stand
- Would I panic if HMRC decided to do a compliance check

If the answer is "no panic", you are ready.

The weekly habit that makes this work

Quarterly deadlines feel heavy. Weekly habits feel light. That difference matters more than motivation or discipline. When everything is left until the end of the quarter, memory fades, errors multiply, and decisions pile up. You end up reconstructing the past under pressure. A weekly habit avoids that entirely.

Fifteen quiet minutes each week will beat three hours of stressed decision making at quarter end, every time.

. . .

The 15 minute routine

This is not "doing accounts". It is a review loop. You are not aiming for perfection. You are reducing complexity. Each session answers one question: *does this broadly reflect reality?*

Minute 1 to 3, scan the bank feed

Look for anything unfamiliar, duplicated, or uncategorised. You are scanning for obvious problems, not tidying everything.

Minute 4 to 7, fix the obvious

Code uncategorised transactions, correct anything clearly wrong, and attach any receipts you already have. If a receipt is missing, make a note and move on. Do not start hunting.

Minute 8 to 11, open one simple report

Open the profit and loss and ask: does income look sensible, are expenses roughly where I expect, has anything odd appeared.

Minute 12 to 14, think briefly ahead

Is a large bill coming up, is cash tighter than expected, do I need to move money for tax?

Minute 15, stop

This matters. Stopping protects consistency. Drifting

into tinkering makes the habit harder to repeat next week. If you miss a week, do not punish yourself with a catch up marathon. Simply resume next week. The habit survives by staying simple.

What success looks like after 90 days

Success does not mean you love bookkeeping, understand every rule, or have perfect records.Success means you are no longer avoiding your numbers, quarterly updates feel routine, and deadlines no longer cause anxiety.

If you are already late

If you are reading this after your deadline date, do not panic. The same plan still works. Compress it if needed. Even partial preparation reduces stress dramatically.

Calm conclusion

Making Tax Digital does not require heroic admin. It requires one small, repeatable routine that removes unnecessary decisions. Do the access step early. Build the foundations. Then let a short weekly habit do the heavy lifting. When you do that, MTD fades into the background, and that is the point.

End of chapter checklist

✅ I can log into my HMRC online account without stress

✅ I know what I need to connect software to HMRC

✅ I have a 90 day plan with one focus per month

✅ I have separated business or rental money from personal spending

✅ My bank feed and receipt capture are working

✅ I have a weekly 15 minute review habit

✅ I know what "ready" looks like, calm, routine, no panic

The MTD Podcast

By this stage you should understand Making Tax Digital and have the foundations of a working system.

If you would like a structured walkthrough to reinforce it, I've recorded an 8-part audio series that guides you step by step.

Each episode is short, practical, and focused on one key area at a time.

Scan the QR code below to access the series.

17

WHEN TO DIY AND WHEN TO INVOLVE AN ACCOUNTANT

Making Tax Digital creates an awkward but important question:

"How much of this should I do myself?"

I'll answer that honestly, with one caveat. I run an accountancy firm, so yes, I'm biased. But I'm also very clear about when people *don't* need an accountant and that might not be what you expect.

This is a conversation I have all the time.

A client of mine, Jack, once rang me and said, "Justin, I think I can do my own tax return."

My answer was immediate.

"Yes. One hundred per cent, you can."

There was a pause. Then he asked the obvious follow-up.

"So why am I paying you?"

I told him the truth.

"About 20% of what you pay me is for producing the tax return. The rest is for the advice you don't notice at the time;

setting up a company pension, spotting that relevant life cover can be a business expense, helping you structure your remuneration properly so you don't create problems later."

I paused and said something I say a lot.

"If you think the value of an accountant is pressing 'submit', then you don't really understand what you're buying."

Jack got it straight away.

"Right," he said. "I'm paying for your experience — and for you keeping up with best practice so I don't have to."

Exactly.

Making Tax Digital is the hot topic right now, but it's important not to lose sight of why accountants exist in the first place. Good accountants sit at the intersection of business, bookkeeping, compliance, and tax. Software can help with all of those things, but software — at least for now — doesn't replace judgement, experience, or context.

AI gets a lot of attention in this space. As someone who is genuinely interested in technology, I'll be clear: what most people call AI here is machine learning. Useful, powerful, and improving — but it doesn't care about your business, your stress levels, or whether a decision is sensible for *you*. A good accountant does.

One of the things I genuinely dislike about Making Tax Digital is that quarterly updates plus a final declaration mean five submissions a year instead of one. That change alone puts pressure on the profession. There's a real risk that everything we traditionally associate with good accountancy — judgement, insight, experience — gets squeezed by administration.

HMRC has been clear that accountants are expected to

lead the transition into MTD. The problem is that leadership is being asked for at the same time as the workload multiplies.

For most clients, what they actually need from an accountant under MTD boils down to three things.

They need someone who genuinely understands MTD not just the headlines. They need someone who can make, or at least oversee, the submissions. And they need someone who can advise on tax, business decisions, and risk.

That balance matters.

Here's the uncomfortable truth. People who genuinely understand tax, technology, and systems end-to-end are rare. There is a real skills gap emerging. Accountants are being asked to carry more operational responsibility at exactly the point many firms are still adapting themselves.

I saw this play out at a seminar run by a large local accountancy firm. They explained MTD, brought in an expert from a major software provider, and walked their clients through what was coming. Then the final slide appeared.

"Don't worry," they said. "We've got you covered. We'll do all of this for you for a flat fee of £1,000 plus VAT per year."

Roughly a third of the room stood up and walked out.

That moment summed up the problem perfectly. The assumption was that clients don't want to learn and won't engage. Some won't — and for them, a fully managed service makes sense. But many people *can* do a lot of this themselves if the system is designed properly.

My client Tony, who I mentioned earlier in the book, is already a bookkeeping hero on Xero. He'll have no trouble carrying much of the MTD workload. The real challenge isn't people like Tony.

The real challenge is helping someone who has never used accounting software before build the confidence, habits, and systems to operate in a quarterly world.

That's the gap MTD exposes.

And it's the gap this book is trying to close.

So don't ask yourself, "Can I do this myself?"

Most people can.

The better question is, "Should I?"

The answer depends on three things.

- First, risk. How much error can you tolerate before it causes real problems?
- Second, complexity. How many moving parts are there. Multiple income streams, joint ownership, VAT, staff?
- Third, temperament. How do you behave under pressure? Do you stay engaged, or do you avoid things until deadlines loom?

Some people like being close to the numbers. Some people hate it. Some people are fine, until stress kicks in.

None of that is a moral failing. It's just how humans work.

Doing things yourself under MTD works best when your setup is simple, your records are kept regularly, and you don't avoid looking at the numbers. Many sole traders and small landlords fit this category. With good software and a short weekly habit, DIY can work very well.

DIY becomes risky when income sources multiply, when joint ownership enters the picture, when records are historically messy, or when you rely on memory rather than systems. At that point, the cost isn't just time, it's stress. And stress tends to surface at the worst possible moment, when deadlines are close and options are limited.

The most expensive mistake people make is involving an accountant too late. They wait until deadlines loom, records are broken, and anxiety is already high. By then, fixing takes longer, fees rise, and trust is harder to build. Early involvement is calmer, cheaper, and far more effective.

In practice, most people do best with a middle ground. They keep records weekly, use software themselves, and involve an accountant for review, guidance, and submissions. That gives control without overwhelm, and support without dependency. Making Tax Digital suits this model extremely well.

One thing I've learned from working with small businesses, teaching on the government-backed Help to Grow programme, and watching systems succeed and fail is this: finance is an outcome, not a starting point. Good financial results come from clean inputs, predictable processes, and clear outputs. When systems are well designed, errors drop, stress drops, and decision-making improves. When systems are fragile, no amount of clever software saves you.

This is what a modern accountant should help you build.

If you do involve an accountant, use them properly. Give them clean data. Ask system questions, not just tax questions. Be clear about responsibilities and review things regularly. Accountants amplify good systems. They cannot quietly rescue bad ones.

This is exactly how we work at Orange Umbrella. We're not the right fit for everyone. We don't do aggressive tax schemes, and we don't pretend one solution fits all. What we specialise in is helping small businesses and landlords build calm, predictable systems, use technology properly, and reduce risk before it turns into stress. That's why we always start with a conversation — sometimes the right advice is pointing someone elsewhere, and that's fine.

Making Tax Digital doesn't force you to choose between doing everything yourself or handing everything over. It forces clarity about who owns the risk. If you understand the system, keep simple habits, and bring in help where it adds value, MTD becomes manageable.

And manageable is enough.

What to do when Making Tax Digital goes wrong

Things will go wrong. Logins fail. Software breaks. Bank feeds stop. Life gets in the way.

The worst response is silence.

If something goes wrong with your Making Tax Digital submissions, the first step is to tell HMRC. You are not asking for permission or forgiveness. You are creating a record that you tried to engage. HMRC systems log contact, so make a note of who you spoke to, the date, and the time of the call. Make sure you contact the right department. It is pointless speaking to PAYE about MTD. These details matter later if deadlines are missed and penalties are considered. Early contact does not fix the problem on its own, but it changes how the problem is viewed.

The second step is to stop trying to solve complex problems on your own. If you find yourself going round in circles with software, authorisations, or failed submissions, get help sooner rather than later. A short conversation with an accountant who understands MTD systems can save weeks of frustration and prevent small issues turning into penalty points. Penalties do not usually come from one mistake. They build when problems drag on.

MTD does not expect perfection, but it does require engagement.

Engaging early, even when something has gone wrong, almost always leads to better outcomes than waiting and hoping it resolves itself.

End-of-Chapter Checklist

- ✅ I know when DIY works for me
- ✅ I understand when risk increases
- ✅ I know what a modern accountant adds under MTD
- ✅ I feel confident choosing the right level of support
- ✅ I know what to do if something goes wrong

SAMPLE FROM THE SCIENCE OF BUSINESS

If you enjoy this sample then consider buying my other book from Amazon it's called the The Science of Business.

Just visit www.thescienceofbusiness.co.uk and it will take you to my Amazon page. Plus don't forget to leave a review. This is the first half of chapter 7, I hope you enjoy it.

7. The Injured Deer - Everyone is different

"Are you better working individually or in a team?"

I hate this question! Interviewers ask this question but have no idea why they are asking it. Neither the person asking the question nor the person answering it really understands.

You see, I'm an extrovert, so I need people around me to give me my mental energy. That interview question should exist in order to determine a personality type. Sorry, but the vast majority of us just don't have the foggiest. I'm 39 and it is only in the last 5 years I could have made a reasonable attempt at answering the question effectively. That said, I would have been safe anyway, as the interviewer wouldn't have understood why they were asking the question in the first place.

Now bear with me. I'm not going to tell you about magic crystals or the power of the sun giving us superpowers. I'm a man of science, after all, and this chapter will help you understand how your brain works. It will help you to understand others.

Before I start my story, I want you to do something for me. Cross your fingers or your arms. Now try to do it the opposite way. Doesn't that feel odd! Your brain has been wired in a particular way and it prefers doing things in that way. Here is another one: look in a mirror and move your eyes side to side. I'll bet you don't see anything. That's because your brain has filtered out the movement. Your brain is merely making guesses most of the time and then filling in the gaps.

So what does all this mean, and what can we do about it?

My Story of Discovery

Through a networking group, I was offered the opportunity to do a Myers-Briggs test, and about a dozen of us decided to team up. Since we'd clubbed together we were able to secure a great deal for a normally expensive exercise. Included were the test, results, 1-to-1 psychologist assessments, and a follow up training day. A tester came to the office and administered the test to me. The test scores were added up and we were given our results. Terrific, I thought, a load of letters – I was apparently an ESTJ. If I'm being honest, I had been a little sceptical about the whole thing, but little did I know a life changing experience was about to follow.

Next up was a psychologist who came to my office and asked me even more questions. Here's where things became fascinating. She gave me several insights into my personality, including the fact that, although the test measured me as well-organised, in actuality I do not tend to be adept at organisation skills. It's only because my powers of self-control and professional training overcome this tendency to disorganisation that I test as well-organised.

"You're not naturally well organised," she said.

Bang! She was on the money. I use diaries, project management software, lists, etc. to keep myself organised. So my Myers-Briggs result was changed by the psychologist from ESTJ to ESTP. During the same meeting, a question popped into my brain and I blurted it out.

"My wife thinks I'm dead inside as I never cry at films. Am I?"

"Why do you say that?" she asked, laughing.

I explained that I'd recently watched the film *Boy in the Striped Pyjamas* and not a tear was in sight. Through her own flood of tears my wife cried, "There is something wrong with you, you're dead inside!"

Her comment had been bothering me ever since. I could

empathise with the horrible things portrayed on screen, but they couldn't bring me to tears.

"Of course you're not dead inside. In fact, it's completely normal for your personality type, and I can prove it. Your brain is wired more than most others to interpret facts. You score highly on the Myers-Briggs scale in this area. The 2nd World War happened a long time ago so your brain simply tells you there is nothing you can do to change the outcome. Moreover, you're watching a film – your brain perceives a fictional story and finds it hard to relate it to real life. You feel there's simply nothing you can do in the present to help those poor people and the boy in the striped pyjamas."

Wow! This was mind blowing, and there was still more to come..............

Read the rest of the chapter by buying The Science of Business.

I hope you enjoyed reading the sample from my first book, *The Science of Business*. It is a five-star rated book and a practical resource for anyone looking to grow their business with more clarity and confidence.

"Justin Turner has created a resource with very wide appeal, which is highly entertaining, informed, inspiring and stimulating. I'm not sure if another is planned, but I hope to hear more from this talented entrepreneur." - Jessica

OTHER RESOURCES

A few years ago Sunday Times Best Selling Author and speaker Michael Heppell asked me to be a keynote speaker at a conference called Day 17. The talk was called 10 ideas to Save 10% in 10 Minutes. It quickly became a fun little book looking at things that save both time and money.

"A great little read that's full of handy hints to help you get a handle on your costs in life. It's a treasure trove of great ideas and practices!" - Greg

Read it now at: https://amzn.eu/d/07eslQh3

A few years ago I created a business education brand called AskJT. I produce YouTube, podcast, and blog content. My aim is to help businesses run better and smarter, and to support them as they modernise how they operate.

Scan the QR code to find out more.

If you need help from an accountant, you can consider my firm, Orange Umbrella. We do sometimes run at capacity, but we will always be clear about whether we can take you on or point you to someone suitable. www.orangeumbrella.co.uk

Help to Grow

Finally, I mention the government backed Help to Grow programme a few times in this book. If you sign up for the version delivered by Northumbria, you may come across me teaching the finance module. I recommend the programme more broadly, as it is delivered nationally.

https://smallbusinesscharter.org/help-to-grow-management

ACKNOWLEDGMENTS

Just before Christmas I was in the car with my wife Sue, telling her about someone who was working a 60-hour week. She laughed and said, "That's what you do."

Do I?

The problem for me is that work isn't always work. I never do a nine-to-five, but I sort of have Wednesdays off. I'm just not very good at sitting still. When the TV is on and I'm bored, I start to tinker.

The last two books were pretty horrendous for Sue, so I felt I owed her a book without the stress, on a subject I could write with my eyes closed. I didn't tell her until the full draft was written and I was part way through the edit.

But the point is this. You are my rock. You put up with my book-writing obsession, my constant ideas, and my inability to properly switch off. Thank you.

Thank you to the clients who, often without knowing it, shaped this book. The January rush, the last-minute surprises, and the conversations that start with "you're not going to like this..." are the reason this book exists. Seeing the same problems repeat year after year made it clear that Making Tax Digital is not really about tax at all. It's about systems.

Thanks to my team at Orange Umbrella and Abode. You give me the space to think, build, and write. Without you, books like this simply wouldn't happen.

Thank you to anyone reading this who feels uncertain

about Making Tax Digital. If this book removes even a small amount of stress, confusion, or panic, then it has done its job.

Finally, I'll give a brief shout-out to Michael Heppell. Three books in now, which is probably his fault, thanks to the Write That Book programme. Michael, you might need to explain a few things to my wife, Sue.

AUTHOR BIO

I'm a family man, triathlete, and entrepreneur. I struggle to sit still and I'm endlessly curious about how things work. I started my first business in 2003 and, like most business owners, learned the hard way. Plenty of mistakes. Plenty of lessons.

When things go wrong, I tend to look for patterns rather than blame. That habit led me to apply ideas from science and systems thinking to business problems, which became my first book, *The Science of Business*. Later, I wrote *10 Ideas to Save 10% in 10 Minutes* for people feeling squeezed by rising costs and needing practical ways to regain control.

This book was written for landlords and sole traders who feel worn down by constant change, admin, and rules that never seem to arrive with a clear "how". In my day job, I see capable people tripped up not by tax rates, but by systems that are unclear and processes that do not fit real life. The aim here is simple. To replace panic with routines, guesswork with systems, and last minute stress with calm preparation.

I run a small accountancy practice serving the SME

sector and employ nine staff. We use modern cloud systems to make record keeping and reporting practical, not painful. I'm also the Financial Director of a local letting agency and a portfolio landlord, so I live on both sides of the table. Before accountancy, I trained as a computer programmer and ran a web development agency for over ten years. I co-founded the practice with my wife in 2012.

Alongside this, I have taught entrepreneurship, innovation, and digital business at Northumbria University since 2011, including work on the government-backed Help to Grow programme. I was hugely honoured to be asked to deliver a public lecture for Northumbria University. I've also guest lectured on executive MBA programmes and acted as a business mentor to founders at different stages of growth.

Outside work, I'm a mad keen triathlete and spend as much time as possible in our campervan with my wife and two boys, travelling the UK and fitting life around races, mud, and missed turnings.

www.ingramcontent.com/pod-product-compliance
Lightning Source LLC
LaVergne TN
LVHW050933210926
848482LV00013B/600